MARY JO SHARP

LIVING IN TRUTH

CONFIDENT CONVERSATION
IN A CONFLICTED CULTURE

LifeWay Press® Nashville, Tennessee

Published by LifeWay Press® © 2015 Mary Jo Sharp

Item 005727072
ISBN 978-1-4300-4024-8

Dewey decimal classification: 248.843
Subject headings: TRUTHFULNESS AND FALSEHOOD \ CHRISTIAN LIFE \ WOMEN

To order additional copies of this resource, write to LifeWay Church Resources Customer Service; One LifeWay Plaza; Nashville, TN 37234-0113; fax 615.251.5933; phone 800.458.2772; email *orderentry@lifeway.com*; order online at *www.lifeway.com*; or visit the LifeWay Christian Store serving you.

Printed in the United States of America
Adult Ministry Publishing
LifeWay Church Resources
One LifeWay Plaza
Nashville, TN 37234-0152

DEDICATION

To my mom, for taking me on journeys to the library.
My family, for sharing our stories throughout this study.
My friend and colleague, Nancy Pearcey,
for her inspiring work.
As well as for:
Those who struggle with living authentically
Christian in our culture.
Those who struggle with doubt.

You are all greatly loved.

ABOUT THE AUTHOR

Mary Jo Sharp is a former atheist from the Pacific Northwest who thought religion was for the weak-minded. She now holds a Masters in Christian Apologetics from Biola University and is the first woman to become a Certified Apologetics Instructor through the North American Mission Board of the Southern Baptist Convention. A clear communicator with a teacher's heart, Mary Jo finds great joy in discussing the deep truths of her Lord and Savior.

CONTENTS

INTRODUCTION

God has called us to the fun, frightening, challenging, and critical task of representing Him to the people of our day and culture. We get to give a reasoned response to explain the hope we have in Christ, and we get to do it with courtesy and gentleness. The task really involves two parts—information content and conversation skills.

The first part most people think about is the information. So when you pick up a book on apologetics it may be filled with complex logical arguments for the existence of God and the truths of the Christian faith. But I consider the second part more important.

In fact, if you grasp the second element, you will be able to relax and enjoy conversations with people. In the process you will pick up the information that will help you to be effective in communicating your faith. You will find *Living in Truth* contains some of the information to help you get started, but our focus will be on the skills to have good conversations—especially asking good questions that help us to share the responsibility of the conversation with the other person.

Simply put I want you to be equipped to relax and enjoy conversations. If another person knows more about a subject than you do, then learn from them. You don't have to win arguments or make converts. That's the Holy Spirit's job. You will achieve much more for the kingdom of Christ by loving people and striving to understand them. You can ask good questions. You can help your friends think through their belief systems. Apologetics is not a battle against unbelievers where you must do the fighting. It is a quest for truth where you get to assist people in their journey. Thank you for allowing me to share the journey.

Speaking of sharing the journey, we live in an exciting time of communication. Our journey can continue beyond the pages of *Living in Truth*. So I am continuing to put up resources and have conversations with you through my website. Check in at *www.maryjosharp.com* to share your comments, find additional helps for your group meetings, and keep the conversation alive.

You will find some distinct components in our study. The main flow of the content will center on how to have good conversations. This process involves developing skills, not merely understanding content. So please do the activities. Write your answers. Talk to friends or group members through the process. Practice the skills in conversation. Real learning involves doing. So take the brave step outside your comfort zone to have the conversations.

Many times I want to see how someone else really plays the instrument or practices the skill. So we've added an element to show you real conversations. Through actual tweets or Facebook postings, you'll see bits of real conversations I've had with skeptics. I hope they'll both illustrate how to courteously engage in apologetics and give you some ideas of how to improve your skills.

Because we've deliberately concentrated on the *how* of good conversations rather than the information, we've included another bonus feature. You'll find a few rather in-depth articles about specific subjects like the sacred/secular split or scientism. You don't have to read these articles, and don't let them scare you. You don't have to have the answers to have good conversations. You just have to care and ask good questions. But you will discover that as you engage people, you will begin to gain far more mastery of the ideas than you thought possible.

Because my concerns are practical, I encourage you to do *Living in Truth: Confident Conversations in a Conflicted Culture* as a group study. Meet with your friends to study together. Ask each other questions. Practice to develop conversation skills. I have given you activities throughout the weeks of study that encourage you to have conversations. The more you practice, the greater your results will be.

You will also find each week begins with two group pages that contain suggestions for your group meeting. You don't have to answer all the questions. This isn't a test. The questions are there so you can be prepared to help each other. Just as playing an instrument, the more you practice, the more results you will see.

Thank you for caring about the struggle for truth. The stakes couldn't be greater. Most of all, you can do it. You can help people come to know the Truth—and His name is Jesus.

Mary Jo Sharp

SEE THE NEED

GROUP

KEY CONCEPTS THIS WEEK:
  1) the need to discuss the truth of our beliefs
  2) areas in our lives infiltrated by falsehood
  3) Jesus' words of loving the truth for our public Christian witness

QUESTIONS FOR DISCUSSION:

1) How has Nietzsche's view that no correct way to live exists affected our culture?

2) What reactions have you received when talking to people about God?

3) What is your definition of truth? Why is truth particularly important to the Christian?

4) What did Eve wrongly believe in Genesis 3:1-11? How did she come to the conclusion, and what were the consequences of her belief?

5) What parallels do you see between Pilate's response to Jesus in John 18:28-38 and our society's response to Jesus?

6) What is the difference between hearing and obeying Jesus vs. affirming correct ideas about Him? Do you see any area in your own life in which you affirm the correct ideas about Jesus but may not necessarily hear and obey Him?

7) In 1 Corinthians 13:6, what does it mean to "rejoice with the truth"?

8) What daily influences do you have to battle to avoid a skewed view of the truth of Jesus? What do you do to combat these influences on your mind?

CALL TO ACTION:

Our society has a lot to say about truth, evidence, and reason. However, those are the very things that seem to be most lacking in conversation. To help you share what you are learning in this study post any of the following statements to your social media sites with hashtags like "Jesus," "truth," and "love" if you want more people to see your posts. Tag me if you want to be retweeted or shared! @maryjosharp #LivingInTruth

In the Scripture, Jesus transparently refers to Himself as the actual truth about the way to heaven. #LivingInTruth

Jesus, himself, is a "curb in the road" for those who say many paths lead to heaven or all beliefs about God are equally true. #LivingInTruth

We are easily persuaded by the untruths of our culture because we have failed to recognize that we are actually surrounded by garbage. #LivingInTruth

Eve exchanged God's truth for a "truth" of her own creation (Rom. 1:23). #LivingInTruth

To be effective in communicating the goodness and truth of Jesus' message to others, we must first commit ourselves to discovering truth. #LivingInTruth

As our society becomes increasingly skeptical about the existence of truth, we cannot expect them to listen to us until they see that we are genuine lovers of the truth. #LivingInTruth

We are the verbal and visual representatives of Christ. #LivingInTruth @maryjosharp

Humans tend to love truth (and the search for it) when it supports what we already want to be true. #LivingInTruth @maryjosharp

The battle for truth is not just between the Christian and the culture/world, it starts between a Christian and her own mind. #LivingInTruth @maryjosharp

I will not squeeze my mind into the mold of the culture. #LivingInTruth @maryjosharp

We live in a time when it has become difficult to discuss belief in God in our society. Why? Many factors may contribute, but a prominent reason is that our society has steadily grown more skeptical that such a thing as truth exists. Yet, in our daily conversations and lives, most people will not explicitly say, "I'm not sure that truth exists." The people we encounter more likely will have been influenced by their culture much more subtly—even subconsciously—to believe that no one has the truth. They will have a hard time articulating why they don't believe in truth or that they don't believe truth exists. Rather, they will use cultural catch phrases, "We should be tolerant;" "Don't be a hater;" "Everyone has their own way;"and "Who are you to judge?"

We see the effects of the skepticism about truth in our culture through many different words and actions. We might hear a song that says the truth is found in each person's heart or watch a movie in which the main character struggles not to find what is true but rather to be true to whatever they desire. Another effect is the view of Christians and of their commitment to the truth of Jesus Christ. You may hear derogatory statements such as:

"Christians are such an ignorant bunch of people. Their ignorance is deeply rooted in arrogance. There are so many different beliefs in the world and yet if you talk to a Christian they will say that only their belief about God is true! They don't respect the views or beliefs of other people. And why do they think they have the truth? Faith ... and faith alone."[1]

Confusion in our culture can stifle a Christian from discussing her belief about God before she even gets started. So our goal for this study is to help every Christian effectively communicate truth by following six basic steps:

1) see the need for truth conversations
2) know whom you trust as an authority
3) listen to discover cultural views
4) learn to ask questions
5) respond to false beliefs
6) live in truth

In Scripture, we are commanded, "Don't be childish in your thinking, but be infants in regard to evil and adult in your thinking" (1 Cor. 14:20). When faced with deceptive philosophies (Col. 2:8), we are supposed to be those who speak words of truth that, through Jesus Christ, can free people from false beliefs. Our world needs a commitment from Christians to be those who are lovers of the truth.

Let's begin our time together by establishing the need to discuss truth with others.

• • • • •

CONVERSATION GOAL: To aptly communicate the importance of truth in the Christian faith and in human lives

Friedrich Nietzsche, an atheist philosopher from the 19th century, wrote: "'This—is now MY way,—where is yours?' Thus did I answer those who asked me 'the way.' For THE way—it doth not exist!"[2] Nietzsche taught the idea that no correct "way" to go exists in this life. He believed each of us creates our own way (or truth) and lives life in accordance with whatever we believe.

Nietzsche's views, as well as those of other notable philosophers, have wreaked havoc on the understanding of truth in Western culture. Many people today, even Christians, are uncertain as to whether truth exists at all. Some of us have become accustomed to the idea that, "Whatever you believe is true for you, and whatever I believe is true for me."

Ultimately, Nietzsche's view denies the existence of

truth, therefore making the search for truth unnecessary. Thus, as Nietzsche inferred, the truth—or the way—becomes whatever a person makes it to be.

Nietzsche's view is unlivable because no matter what we believe, we still crash into truth every day of our lives. The late Christian philosopher, Dallas Willard, said, "Reality is what we … run into when we are wrong."[3] Though sometimes I try to create my own way, I can assure you that I regularly "run into" reality.

Think of how truth affects your daily life. Describe a time when you found out you were wrong on something you believed or you took an action based on a wrong belief.

What was it that was wrong?

After discovering the untruth, did you adjust your thinking? Why or why not?

What was the consequence of your wrong thinking?

If you had trouble with the exercise, you may be thinking too narrowly about beliefs. Everything we do is based on our beliefs. Think of a time when you were mistaken about any practical issue of life. Then go back and complete the activity.

You've probably never conceptualized it this way, but running into reality can be like an experience I had in my truck. One day, I was driving along a familiar route. I wasn't paying especially careful attention. I had allowed the routine to lull me into a false sense of security. Suddenly, out of the blue, I hit a piece of curb protruding from a construction zone. The entire vehicle shook. I think even my teeth rattled. Reality can be very solid, and it can hurt.

Similarly, every day we go along a familiar route or, as Nietzsche described, go our own way, guided by the beliefs we have casually picked up. Few of us stop to ask how we know what we think we know or to examine whether our beliefs are true. Rather, we simply accept the life assumptions of those around us. We allow cultural views of truth to lull us into inattentiveness.

The trouble is we will all run into reality at points along the way, and on the most serious life issues, reality will hurt far worse than a road hazard. In this study we seek to build the skills to help people confront their false beliefs before the obstacles become devastating. When we engage people in conversation about God, we are essentially acting as a curb for them to run into. We do so to prevent them from continuing until they smash into a granite mountain.

Name one reaction people usually give when they run into an unexpected obstacle.

What are some of the reactions you have received when talking to people about God? You may include reactions from Christians and non-Christians.

Imagine you could see what was going on in their mind. Why do you suppose they reacted this way?

When a person has accepted the idea that no truth exists in religious beliefs, they may also believe that it's inappropriate to discuss belief in God in public. It's like discussing your dirty laundry at a ladies' tea, or trotting out marital problems at your cousin's wedding. So when you begin to share your belief in God as not only real, but something that actually matters in everyday life, you may give a person quite a shock. If they have believed no God exists (or that Jesus is not God), and have lived accordingly, to be told that they may be wrong can be quite jarring.

Therefore, one of our goals in conversation about belief in God is to demonstrate the importance of truth within the Christian faith. Our belief must ultimately be grounded in truth or our belief is of no real consequence. Our first step must be to understand what we mean by truth.

What is truth? Without looking it up, write your own definition.

What we know to be true → something I don't have to question

This week sometime, get together with two or three people. Share your responses to the question and inquire about how they would define truth. Or you can compare your response to a dictionary definition, but what's the fun in that? Engaging people in conversation is challenging, but it can be joyful.

The definition of truth can be expressed many ways. We're going to use a definition that helps us communicate our belief in God clearly: truth is "telling it like it is." So, for example, if I say the grass is purple when it is actually green, I've said something false. If I say the grass is purple and it really is purple, then I've said something true (wouldn't that be great … purple grass!). However, notice that my statement is true or false. One would not say in response, "No truth exists about the color of the grass," or "Whatever anyone believes is true about the grass is what is true for them." These statements would be absurd.

When we talk to people and we say, "Jesus is God," we believe we are "telling it like it is." The statement is either true or false. We are either "telling it like it is" or we are not. Just like the grass example, it would be absurd for someone to say, "There is no truth as to whether Jesus is God," or "Whatever anyone believes is true about Jesus is true for them."

Why would it be absurd for someone to say, "There is no truth about the color of the grass"?

BC their is a truth - we can all see that grass a color and agree what color it is.

Why would it be absurd for someone to say, "There is no truth about whether Jesus is God"?

BC Jesus is god -

When we tell people that we believe in the truth of Jesus Christ, we mean to say that we believe this is the way things are. Further, if our belief is true, some obvious implications result. Going back to my earlier story, I can believe the road has no curb if that belief makes me feel good. However, my belief does not change reality, nor will my good feelings or beliefs in any way mitigate the repair bills for fixing my vehicle. You see, my belief must match reality to be true.

What question does Thomas ask Jesus in John 14:1-6?

How do we know how to get to Jesus/heaven?

What is Jesus' reply?

"I am the way, the truth, the light. no one comes to the Father except thru me"

In the Scripture, Jesus transparently refers to Himself as the actual truth about the way to heaven. Jesus, Himself, is a "curb in the road" for those who say many paths lead to heaven or all beliefs about God are equally true. Jesus drew a spiritual line in the sand to say no other way leads to life now, or ever, except through His offer of salvation.

To a world that wants to find its own "way," Jesus' words can feel like smashing into a very solid wall. For some, the hit will shake them up and wake them up. For others, they will continue to zone out to the truth—perhaps because they are comfortable in their routine. Yet, they will not be able to avoid the very real consequences of denying Jesus as the salvation of God.

Why does truth matter to the Christian?

BC the truth is the only way to salvation.

Why should truth matter to everyone?

BC everyone should WANT to be w/ Jesus

How can you communicate the importance of truth when discussing your beliefs?

Unfortunately, many Christians never stop to examine their beliefs. Most of us give our faith serious thought and attention only when crashes force us to think about reality. Otherwise, we drift along, blindly adopting the beliefs of those around us. We only seem to get shaken out of our lethargy when we come into contact with something that rocks our world.

Let's take a moment to thank God for being the Author of Truth. Begin to pray for those around you who need to examine the reality of truth.

As we go through this study together, I encourage you to collect the verbal gift cards. They are carefully crafted statements you can use to keep conversations on track and positive. Copy them, and carry them with you. Use them as tools for productive conversations.

VERBAL GIFT CARD: "I am committed to searching for the truth as much as possible in one lifetime. Though I know sometimes I will fail, I believe this is basic part of being a Christian since Jesus Christ said He was the Way, the Truth, and the Life."

CONFIDENCE BUILDER: Definitions of Truth

Here are a couple of other ways of stating the definition:

1) A belief or statement is true only if it matches with, reflects, or corresponds to the reality to which it refers;

2) Truth is "the property (as of a statement) of being in accord with fact or reality;"[4] or

3) The Greek philosopher Aristotle's definition, "To say of what is that it is not, or of what is not that it is, is false, while to say of what is that it is, and of what is not that it is not, is true; so that he who says of anything that it is, or that it is not, will say either what is true or what is false."[5] (Give yourself a little pat on the back for reading an ancient Greek philosopher!) We're using a definition of truth related to the "Correspondence Theory of Truth." Other theories concerning truth exist, but we will be relying upon the correspondence theory throughout this study. In relation to our conversations about belief in God, the correspondence theory tells us that if we say Jesus is the Savior and Creator of all things, and that statement matches the way things really are, then the statement is true.

CONVERSATION GOAL: To communicate that our beliefs have consequences

False beliefs litter our culture. The situation is so bad that it reminds me of the garbage compactor scene in the movie, *Star Wars*. Every day, I feel like the character Luke Skywalker wading through piles of false belief trash with the walls closing in on me. Trudging through such a huge pile of garbage is slow going and takes tremendous purposeful effort to not get trapped. Yet that is the task immediately before us: not only must we find a way out of the garbage, but we have to help others get out of that garbage, too! (Remember, Luke was in there with Han Solo, Princess Leia, and Chewbacca.)

What kind of false belief garbage is floating around in our society? Just take a moment to think about the commercials and ads in our society and you'll find a myriad of untruths such as:

- Beauty resides in fashion, youth, and tight abs.
- We deserve luxuries like fine dining, sports cars, and exotic vacations.
- Security in life can be monetized (you can put a dollar value on it).
- The most important thing in life is following your individual desires and dreams.
- What you believe doesn't matter as long as you are sincere.

In bestselling books, popular science shows, sitcoms, political campaigns, and Internet blogs we are further exposed to untruths such as:

- To be good we don't need God.
- Science is the only way to know truth.
- To be Christian is to commit intellectual suicide.
- Belief in God is antiquated.

What are some actions that may result from the first group of beliefs?

living beyond our means trying to be someone I am not

What are some actions that may result from the second group?

to ignore god totally

Can you think of other false beliefs in our society? Please take time to list some.

What results from those false beliefs?

As a result of false beliefs, people focus their lives on so many things other than discovering what is true. As authors Francis Schaeffer and Allan Bloom noted, our society has become focused on fulfilling our own pleasures to the extent that we have abandoned a serious life of the mind.[6] We are easily persuaded by the untruths of our culture because we have failed to recognize that we are actually surrounded by garbage. Then we live according to those false beliefs.

That's one reason why we see a society chasing after personal peace and affluence rather than seeking out the answers to difficult questions about life. Garbage, aka false beliefs, have become truths to us, since we are all finding our own way, as Nietzsche described.

In the *Star Wars* scene, if Luke hadn't recognized the actual truth of his situation, the garbage compac-

tor would have squeezed the life out of him. Similarly, our beliefs—both true and false—have consequences, which is why it is so vital to look at what a person believes and the truth of those beliefs.

What did Eve wrongly believe in Genesis 3:1-11?

That if she ate fruit of forbidden tree she'd be like god.

How did she come to this conclusion?

Satan told her that

What was the consequence of her belief?

She and Adam realized they were naked - hid from god

In this story, we see that Eve exchanged God's truth for a truth of her own creation (Rom. 1:23). The result was that Eve accepted a false belief: that the fruit of the tree would be good for her. When she had acted on that belief, she reaped more false knowledge and beliefs.

Notice that when God speaks to Adam and Eve, they tell Him that they are hiding in fear because they are naked. God asks them, "Who told you that you were naked?" The implication is that Adam and Eve have gained false beliefs; one of which was a negative connotation of nakedness. If the two humans who were closest to God could act out of false beliefs, then certainly we do so today.

In our study together I'm going to ask you to take some difficult steps—to stop and examine your own beliefs. I know this is challenging, but sometimes we can grow only through difficult self-examination.

What is something that either you or a friend believe about God/church/Christianity that may just be a cultural thing and not a biblical truth?

? Judging?

How do you think people acquire this belief?

What are some actions you, or a friend, have taken in accordance with that belief?

Did that series of questions give you trouble? Such self-examination can feel a bit like trying to crawl outside ourselves to get an objective look. But living in truth requires such difficult work.

While we do no good by beating ourselves up over the past, we can determine to change the future. To be effective in communicating the goodness and truth of Jesus' message to others, we must first commit ourselves to discovering truth.

In the following two days of study, we will reflect on what Jesus and Paul had to say about Jesus' followers. We will discover a need to commit to truth, not just as a profession of faith for salvation, but as a moment-by-moment striving in our daily lives. Our purpose is for the sake of others. We begin with our own understanding of truth so that we can communicate trust in God to the world around us.

Let's wrap up today by looking at some false belief garbage that may be floating around in our minds. See if any of these statements sound familiar:

✳ "Religion is a private matter."

"It's not appropriate to talk about God."

"If I don't see a conversion in this person, I haven't been effective."

✳ "People don't like to talk about God."

"The ministers are supposed to talk to people about God, not me."

✳ "I don't have the gift of evangelism (in regard to daily conversation)."

✳ "It's always awkward to talk about belief in God."

Do you believe any of these statements? If you do, you're not alone. I've heard these statements in many of the places at which I have spoken.

What actions will probably result from believing any one of these to be true?

I won't have a conversation about God w/ others

If you believe any of these, you are probably hindered in speaking to people about God on a daily basis. I don't mean to say you wouldn't do evangelism pushes or even be evangelistic for some time. Rather, if there is a falsehood in your mind about conversations, then you'll eventually go back to your habits formed over time by that belief. These beliefs will literally squeeze the life out of your conversations.

We are currently living out what we believe and those beliefs may be hindering our ability to share the truth. My hope is that by the end of our time together you will be encouraged like Abraham who was "fully convinced that God was able to do what he had promised" (Rom. 4:21, ESV). At the very least, if you are encouraged to look back at your beliefs to see why you haven't been freely discussing God as part of natural, daily conversation, then we have achieved much.

WORD OF ENCOURAGEMENT: Much freedom comes from learning to "trust in the Lord with all your heart, and do not rely on your own understanding " (Prov. 3:5).

DAY THREE

CONVERSATION GOAL: To value truth in our everyday matters and everyday life

Are you a person who is "of the truth"? This question rattled around in my mind as I flew to a conference in San Diego. I'd never gone to a church that taught on this subject. I've always been in churches where "truth" was assumed or taken for granted. I remember when I began to question why I believed in God, I uncovered a serious problem: I didn't know why I believed it was true that Jesus rose from the dead. Nor did I know why I thought a myriad of other beliefs were true.

From my experiences with other Christians, I encountered many people who could say that Jesus was "the truth," but they didn't much act like it. This apparent hypocrisy caused me to have doubts about my own belief in God. So I set out on a journey to discover the facts about Jesus and Christianity.

As I began to look at the objections against and the arguments for the Christian faith, I came to the conclusion that the claim, "Jesus Christ rose from the dead," is intellectually defensible. That personal journey led me into my field of study—apologetics.

CONFIDENCE BUILDER: Apologetics—a Koine Greek word, transliterated from the New Testament text. It means to give or make a defense. In the context of my field of study, the word means specifically to make a case for belief in the Christian God, which includes answering objections to belief in God.

What I didn't expect in my journey was that I would begin to discover more than just the facts. I began to uncover a Person who is truth; a Person I can only know if I am "of the truth."

My belief in God was transforming from a line of flat facts and traditions towards a fully rounded relationship with a person. Twice, I was shocked at what I discovered. First, I found the evidence and reason to substantiate my belief in God. Second, I found deeper intimacy with God as I began to know Him as the Lord of Truth … my true King.

What is the first question Pilate asks of Jesus in John 18:28-38?

Are you king of Jews

How does Jesus respond?

Do you ask on your own, or did others tell you about me.

How does Jesus describe His kingship?

"My kingdom is not from here"

What is Jesus' purpose on earth?

to testify to the truth

How does Pilate respond to Jesus' purpose?

what is the truth?

Why do you think Pilate responded this way?

The Jewish leaders brought Jesus before Pilate asking him to enact the punishment of execution. These leaders made multiple accusations against Jesus including that Jesus claimed to be a king. However, they didn't know His kingdom. Why? Because they were not "of the truth" and therefore did not "listen to his voice." This part of the passion story is so familiar that we might miss a powerful indictment here. These very religious people (leaders), honored and respected by the people as experts in the Torah, were, in fact, not "of the truth."

1

CONFIDENCE BUILDER: It can be difficult in our day to speak to skeptics of the truth of the Christian faith, in part, due to quick access to the Internet. We may share with a person about Jesus' sacrificial love, yet that person can quickly find an online story of a Christian leader who has been publicly disgraced. It is hard to express that some professed Christian leaders are Christian in name only and are not those who are of the truth, such as these very religious leaders in Jesus' day. It is also difficult to express that some professed Christian leaders actually are Christians trusting in God who have failed greatly in their commitment to love truth.

How does Jesus describe His followers in John 18:37?

Everyone who belongs to the truth

Jesus' followers are not necessarily anyone who can talk about Jesus and God or quote Scripture, rather they are those who listen to and obey His voice, those who are of the truth. I'd like to think that I am a person who is truthful, a person who is also concerned with what is true. Therefore, I think it is important to explore what we mean when we say, "of the truth." I know when I talk to some of my friends and the word *truth* is mentioned I see eyes begin to glaze over. (They probably figure I'm going to bring up some movie reference from *Lord of the Rings* or *Star Wars*.) However, I understand their eye-glaze since truth is quite an abstract concept. We cannot physically point to a truth in the way we might point at a beautiful sunset or waterfall, saying, "See! There's truth. Isn't it beautiful?"

So even after defining truth (Day One), we may have difficulty wrapping our minds around the meaning of it. Yet, Jesus was emphatic that His followers were of the truth.

To help us clarify our thinking on this important subject, look back at Jesus' statement:

JESUS SAID, "EVERYONE WHO IS OF THE TRUTH LISTENS TO MY VOICE" (JOHN 18:37).

What do you think this statement means? Be ready to discuss your answer with your group.

Everyone who knows the truth AND obeys

Why do you think Jesus replied to Pilate in this way?

Be there are those who know the truth but choose not to obey

How does His statement apply to us today? What personal applications of the statement can you make?

There are many who know the truth but don't obey - listening doesn't just mean to HEAR. Must also follow

Jesus, after pronouncing that His mission on earth was to testify to truth, makes the claim that those who are of the truth listen to His voice. The word *listen* in this passage does not just refer those who hear Jesus but to those who actively obey. As *The New American Commentary* says, "Truth is related to ideas and matters of facticity, but Jesus' mission was to bring people to himself and to God and in the process thereby bring them to integrity of life. It is clearly possible to be academically right and theologically correct but still lack integrity in life. Jesus' mission was to integrate truth into life. That is the reason the text here defines people who are of truth as those who hear the voice of Jesus. Hearing or obeying Jesus is not the same as affirming correct ideas."[7]

What is the difference between hearing and obeying Jesus and affirming correct ideas about Jesus? *It's one thing to know what is right and another to do the right thing!*

Do you see any area in your own life in which you affirm the correct ideas about Jesus but may not necessarily hear and obey Him? Write a few of them here: *all the time! I know what I should do, but often fail. Judging others!*

What does the commentary mean by "bring them into integrity of life"? *doing "right" b/c it's what I want to do, not bc it's what I think I'm supposed to do.*

To be the kind of people who can effectively tell it like it is, we must first commit to matching our lives up to the truth of Jesus Christ, not just commit to proclaiming what is true. As we saw in Day Two, this is not an easy task, in part, due to the cultural untruths influencing our minds and, in part, due to our own lack of disciplining our minds. As our society becomes increasingly skeptical about the existence of truth, we cannot expect them to listen to us until they see that we are genuine lovers of the truth.

If we want to have effective conversations about God with our friends, neighbors, colleagues, and family, we must first understand the life of integrity to

which Jesus has called us. One of the most difficult aspects of my own Christian faith is trying to hear the truth of Jesus Christ and obey Him even in the small matters of life, in those everyday activities and small talk that demonstrate my ultimate belief in the truth of the gospel of Jesus Christ. We are the verbal and visual representatives of Christ. Our lives speak to the integrity of the gospel message. We must be those who are "of the truth" if we desire to speak the truth in love. *LIVE IT!*

DAY FOUR

CONVERSATION GOAL: To discover if we are lovers of truth and to determine how we demonstrate that love in our conversations

In 1 Corinthians 13:6, what does it mean to "rejoice in the truth"? *"does not rejoice in wrongdoing, but rejoices in the truth" wants to do what is right – happy to be doing what is right.*

In Paul's letter to the Corinthians, the apostle describes various attributes of love, and one of the attributes is how love relates to truth. As *The Baker New Testament Commentary* describes, "Love and truth are inseparable partners residing in God himself ... God shares these characteristics with his people. He endowed them with love and truth, which, though tainted by sin, are renewed in Christ Jesus through the indwelling of the Holy Spirit."[8] If we truly love God, then we are supposed to rejoice when people, including ourselves, are living in accordance with truth.

Though we were created to live in truth, we sometimes act on false beliefs, from which we may have even formed habits. So let's take a moment to think on God's call to love truth.

Do you love truth? What evidence would you say demonstrates to others that you do?

I try to. I try to make godly decisions.

What evidence might suggest you don't love truth?

There are times that either I make bad choices, or do the right thing but not w/ a happy heart.

Do you want as much truth as possible? Why or why not?

Of course I want as much truth as possible! Having & living truth has me that much closer to god.

Have you become complacent in your thought life (or some areas of your thought life), not allowing for the discovery of truth? Explain your answer.

Absolutely! I'm LAZY! It's not that I don't want to discover the truth – I just don't want to have to think abt it!

Though I've asked some similar questions earlier, think again on this: *Are you open to the suggestion that you may be wrong in some areas, or even in many areas?*

Over many years in ministry, I've never met a person who's said, "I don't want truth! I want as much false-hood as I can get!" However, commenting on the human condition, Saint Augustine said, "They love truth for the light it sheds, but hate it when it shows them up as being wrong."[9] *AMEN!*

We humans tend to love truth (and the search for it) when it supports what we already want to be true. So getting to the point that we actually love and rejoice in truth, even when it's not what we desire, is a much more difficult, even painful, task.

As you can see, the battle for truth is not just between the Christian and the culture/world, it starts between a Christian and her own mind. The first step towards loving truth is acknowledging our own failure in this area. We must take a deep look at what we are letting into our minds, what we allow to influence our thinking. Many things daily contribute to a skewed view of the truth of Jesus Christ.

Name some daily influences that you have to battle to avoid a skewed view of the truth of Jesus in your mind: *listening to others negativity*

What do you do to combat these influences on your mind?

A few ways you can combat influences that skew truth include:

- Determine what is actually being said or shown, not just what you thought you heard or saw. (We'll work on this in Week Three.)
- Examine whether you have good reason to believe the truth or falsity of the influence.
- Evaluate the source of the influence—does that source demonstrate a commitment to truth?
- Consider how this concept might negatively affect your thoughts.
- Determine how this influence might positively affect your thoughts.

By just taking a little time on a daily basis to think about the visual and audio influences that we have encountered, we can see much improvement in our own commitment to loving and living in truth.

Not everything we encounter is like our *Star Wars* trash compactor garbage, but it takes a concerted effort to wade through it all. The apostle Paul further commented on how we can learn to analyze what we see and hear.

What does Romans 12:2 mean by the command to conform to something?

What does Paul mean by the term "this age" (or "this world")?

How does a person conform to "this age"?

Paul warned the believers in Rome that they are not to be molded or formed by the philosophies, methodologies, fashions, and culture of the fallen world in which they were living. We have already seen that the culture of our time can create in us so many false beliefs. These beliefs lead to ruin, not to truth—no matter how sincerely they are practiced. However, as Paul recognized, we must choose to no longer allow these untruths to influence our minds.

What do you think it means to "be transformed"?

In accordance with the Scripture, how is a person supposed to be transformed?

Discuss the term *renewing of the mind*. What is it and how do you do it?

What is the purpose of renewing the mind?

Transformation means to undergo a change in form, appearance, or character. In Romans, Paul described that a person experiences this change through a constant renewing of his or her mind.

In looking at various definitions for *renewing,* one word struck me: *repairing.* Our minds have been greatly influenced—damaged—by the world with all of its falsehoods. Renewing the mind is like repairing the damage caused by false beliefs. J.B. Phillips translated this passage as "do not let the world squeeze you into its mold."[10]

Think of what happens when you try to squeeze something into a mold of which it is not intended to fit. Typically, you damage the original item. Now think of how your mind is damaged when you try to conform it to worldly ideas. Paul implies a specific damage here, which leaves the person with an inability to discern what is good and evil.

VERBAL GIFT CARD: "I'm trying not to squeeze my mind into the mold of our culture. I desire to be a lover of the truth."

①

Name one thing that our culture says is good, which is actually not good:

Many examples show our culture's inability to discern good and evil. One recent idea that has flipped takes us from thinking belief in God is good to the view that belief in God may be evil. Oxford professor Richard Dawkins has spoken about this belief when he stated that teaching your child to believe is "child abuse."[11]

How might your conversation about belief in God be affected if someone believes religion is like child abuse?

What could you say or do to respond to such a belief?

Do you think you've been influenced in any way by the idea that belief in God may be bad for a person? If so, how? If not, why do you think the idea hasn't influenced you?

Before I became a Christian, I was greatly influenced by the idea that religion may be a bad thing. I didn't really spend time thinking about this idea nor did I even realize it was one of the influencers in my thought life. However, I did know that I had an unexamined distrust of the church institution and felt a little weird around devoutly religious people. I had conformed to the world in this area. I was squeezing my mind into the mold of the culture.

When Paul tells us to renew (or repair) our minds, he means we must daily give attention to the truth. We must be those who love the truth, imbibing it deeply and often. For if we profess to follow Jesus, then we must be those who treasure goodness and truth, rejecting what is evil. In Luke 6:45, we find Jesus saying, "The good person out of the good treasure of his heart produces good, and the evil person out of his evil treasure produces evil, for out of the abundance of the heart his mouth speaks." Thus, as we are abundantly filled with the love of truth, so also should we deeply desire to speak of this truth to others.

CONFIDENCE BUILDER: Have you ever had a person imply that because you are Christian you are not a reliable source for truth? I have heard and read this many times in my conversations with atheists and Muslims. There is a problem with this statement: It commits an error in reasoning called a *genetic fallacy*. The genetic fallacy is a logical error made when someone discredits an argument or view based on the source of the argument, rather than on the argument's merit or truth. Granted, at times the source of an idea could be a problem, such as if you're quoting an article from *The Onion* without knowing it is a satirical news source. However, a wholesale rejection of a person's view solely based on the fact that it comes from that person is a genetic fallacy. We often commit these errors during political campaigns with statements like, "You can't trust them, they are a right-wing republican/left-wing democrat." These genetic fallacies do not help us get to the truth. In fact, these errors generally lead us away from truth.

DAY FIVE

CONVERSATION GOAL: To be committed to the truth in our everyday lives so we can have better conversations

In this first week together, we've covered some of the reasons why truth is so important to our lives as Christians and with regard to our conversations with others.

Think back through the reasons you've learned and write them in your own words:

1)

2)

3)

4)

Which one of the above reasons has most impacted you this week?

Why did that reason impact you?

Can you think of any other reasons for why studying truth is so important to our conversations? Be ready to discuss your answers.

A concept like "truth" seems deceptively simple. We should just be able to say "truth is telling it like it is," and yet when Christians engage others in "telling it like it is" we sometimes meet with much resistance and even, at times, hostility. So this concept—truth—involves much more than what we see at face value.

When we begin to share the truth of Christianity with others, we must remember Pilate's question, "What is truth?" We face a culture with many, and oftentimes conflicting, responses to Pilate's words. We desire to share Jesus as the truth with the world, and yet the world does not know if there is any truth to be found, especially regarding God. Instead of getting discouraged, remember Jesus' response in John 18:37, "I was born for this, and I have come into the world for this: to testify to the truth. Everyone who is of the truth listens to My voice."

How does knowing Jesus has come to testify to truth encourage you in conversations about God? Or does it? Why or why not?

For me, knowing that Jesus' purpose was to testify to the truth combined with knowing reasons for why I believe Him to be telling the truth (why I believe in God) gives me confidence to share His truth. Knowing that what we claim as true really is true provides us with a basis for having confident conversations about truth.

Have you ever considered that influences from our culture may affect your ability to converse with others about belief in God? Explain what those influences might be and how they've affected your ability to talk to non-Christians about your beliefs. Plan to share with your group some thoughts on this matter.

As we finish Week One, I want to take a moment to acknowledge that, realistically, much of what we've allowed into our thoughts over the years has been based in untruth. We have formed images of intellectual authorities, financial wellbeing, power, relationships, sexuality, and beauty that are not based on the teachings of Jesus Christ.

We have so much informing our minds that is not the truth of God that when we are in a situation in which we could speak truth, we may find that we lack knowledge of what to say. My hope in working through this study is that you will discover a renewed and refreshed desire to know the truth—who is a living Person.

From that desire, I pray you will begin to find the freedom in Christ that is already yours to openly discuss your beliefs, no matter how conflicted our culture

becomes. Though, in some places, the study will be packed with apologetic arguments and answers, I've tried to keep in mind along the way that in discussing truth, we are referencing a living being. So our purpose is always relational.

Would you pray for someone right now whom you know is struggling with living in truth?

CONFIDENCE BUILDER: This study is meant as an introduction to the discussion of living in truth. To "live in truth" is a life-long process of transformation to the image of Christ, that is, Christlikeness (2 Cor. 3:18). Many of the truth problems we face are due to our own lack of building relationship with the Lord and allowing Him to guide and direct our lives. No condemnation is intended here. Rather, the intention is to gain a more realistic understanding of our situation.

In combination with a study such as this—or as a follow up—it would be beneficial to do a study on the spiritual disciplines. The disciplines help us trust in God for our individual truth journey. They help to peel away the things on which we've been leaning other than God—those things which effectively pervert the truth in our lives. For further study consider: *Spiritual Disciplines for the Christian Life* by Donald Whitney, *Renovation of the Heart: Putting on the Character of Christ* by Dallas Willard, *Soul Keeper* by John Ortberg.

UPSTAIRS/DOWNSTAIRS:
THE SACRED/SECULAR SPLIT

Some people become upset when you disagree with their ideology or share the gospel with them. They may not even understand the underlying problem of the sacred/secular split.

The line between faith and reason has been thickening since the time of the late medieval thinkers. Approaching the time of the Reformation (1517-1648), they began to slowly separate faith and reason into unrelated categories. Revelation had been seen as a set of truths that could not be contradicted by human reason. These truths were a yardstick for discerning error. Yet by the time of William of Ockham (c.1287-1387), the separation was near the breaking point. Ockham denied that God "could be understood in rational categories at all."

Prior to Ockham, Christian thinkers argued that God's plan of salvation was logical. Yet Ockham was concerned that if "we apply rational principles to God in any way, we deny His absolute freedom." The thinking that resulted held that since religion comes from revelation, it is accepted solely by faith. Theologians split faith and reason into two categories. Complete secularization was only a small step away. "For if virtually everything needed for ordinary life could be known by reason alone, eventually people began to ask why we need revelation at all."

This new view of rationalism shifted the balance of power. Where revelation had been the yardstick for error, now reason became the measure. As the medieval period gave way to the Renaissance (beginning in the 1300s), the idea that reason should be completely "emancipated" from revelation was gaining ground. By the Enlightenment, we see the full force of the argument.

Going beyond the separation of faith and reason, enlightenment thinkers proclaimed human reason the only arbiter of truth. They "enthroned science as the sole source of genuine knowledge...Whatever was not susceptible to scientific inquiry was pronounced an illusion."

The Enlightenment thinking caused a problem: things like morality, art, and beauty cannot be scientifically investigated. In response, later philosophers in the Romantic era tried to "preserve some cognitive territory for things that are not reducible to scientific materialism, including religion, morality, and the arts and humanities." The Romantics conceded the study of nature to mechanistic science while seeking to carve out a "parallel arena for the arts and humanities."

The result was the split view of knowledge we experience in life today. Anything we can know by scientific methods is considered as belonging to the public sphere of verifiable fact. Anything we cannot know through scientific methods is considered part of the private sphere of the mind, and is not considered as fact, but rather value-laden opinion, preference, and social construct.

Francis Schaeffer illustrated the faulty thinking of this split as the lower story versus the upper story of knowledge. The lower story contains science and reason, which are considered public truth. The upper story contains faith, religion, traditions, morality, which are non-rational and considered private truth. We find facts in the lower story. We derive our personal values and meaning in life—but no verifiable facts—from the upper story. Schaeffer saw this two-story view of knowledge as a huge problem. As Nancy Pearcey says, this split is "the single most potent weapon for delegitimizing the biblical perspective the public square today."

This history of philosophical ideas affects us today in at least two devastating ways. First, it hinders the spread of the gospel both as the light of truth and a restrainer of evil. Since many people view religion as upper story knowledge with no verifiable facts, they reject the good news of Jesus as fictitious before investigating its claims. When a Christian attempts to share the truth of Jesus Christ, a person may become offended that you are not respecting his or her privacy. In this view, religion occupies the upper, private realm—not for public debate. When asking about a friend's beliefs, I have been told, "Religion is a personal, private matter."

Moving religion into the upper story, creates the sense that religion is wholly subjective. Therefore, a person may understand "I believe Christianity is true," to mean, "It is my preference to follow Christianity." To help such a person understand that I'm saying Christianity is objectively true becomes a difficult task. If we relegate the gospel to the upper story, then it has no facts concerning what is good and evil for the public realm (the lower story). You may have heard someone get upset about a person bringing their religion into the workplace, school, or politics, as if religious morality has nothing to say in these public places.

The second problem impacts believers. The sacred/secular split has crept into Christians' lives. Some Christians, knowingly or not, also divide their field of knowledge into the upper and lower stories. I have encountered Christians who believe Christianity is true for them, but can be false for someone else. When I ask why they believe this way, I usually receive a response of religion being a private matter. "How can I say what is true for someone else? All I can tell them is what is true for me." Sometimes these Christians are not sure it is appropriate to discuss Christianity as the truth. This is a clear example of the split view of knowledge. Religion, for these folks, is non-verifiable knowledge that belongs to the upper story.

Nancy Pearcey calls this the sacred/secular split, which comes from the split view of knowledge into the two stories. Religious life is bound to the upper story and doesn't interact much, or at all, with the secular life of daily activities that take place as part of the lower story. I've seen many times when Christian friends—even pastors—have shut down conversation on God because they deem the setting to be secular. However, no time or place is inappropriate to discuss the things of God, since life is God's creation.

Christians must grapple with the current thinking that knowledge falls in two realms, because it greatly affects our spiritual lives, as well as our evangelism. As Pearcey explains, "Where we hear the language of 'separate realms,' we can be sure that one of them will be accorded the status of objective truth, while the other is demoted to private illusion."[11] As the upper realm of knowledge is rapidly demoted to the status of being purely subjective, the lower realm will begin to eat up the upper realm, "dissolving away all traditional concepts of morality and meaning."

"Christians cannot afford to promulgate a dichotomized stereotype of Christianity wherein a believer's spiritual life is a private, individualized faith operating in some upper story (to borrow Francis Schaeffer's term) while his secular life is public and involves reason and argument."[12]

FOR FURTHER STUDY

Nancy Pearcey. *Total Truth: Liberating Christianity from Its Cultural Captivity* (Wheaton, IL: Crossway Books, 2005)

Francis Schaeffer. *How Should We Then Live? The Rise and Decline of Western Thought and Culture* (Wheaton, IL: Crossway Books, 1976, 2005)

2

KNOW
WHAT YOU
BELIEVE

GROUP

2

KEY CONCEPTS THIS WEEK:
  1) actively building our on lives on the truth of God's Word
  2) understanding why we trust Jesus as an authority
  3) trusting Jesus as the authority for our conversations about God

QUESTIONS FOR DISCUSSION:

1) On what two bases did those in Jesus' parable (Matt. 7:24-28) build? What happens to the houses, and for what teaching did Jesus use these houses as a metaphor?

2) How would you explain the difference between a person who just hears Jesus' teachings and one who puts them into practice?

3) How does failing to daily build on the foundation of Jesus by practicing His teaching affect our ability to converse with others about God?

4) How can we discern truth if we lack time to individually research all decisions?

5) Why did the people marvel that Jesus taught with authority? Why does His authority make a practical difference for your conversations?

6) What does it take for you to trust a person as an authority? How does your list compare to the one about Jesus? Are there any similarities or differences?

7) If merely knowing and being convinced of the arguments for the existence of God and validity of Scripture would not be sufficient to motivate us to obey and engage in presenting truth, what do you think would motivate us?

8) In the contest of conversation, what does it mean to deny yourself (Matt. 16:24-27)?

9) What are some ways you tend to protect yourself in conversation?

10) When we get defensive or easily angered, what are we communicating about God to the other person in the conversation?

Free video session downloads available at *www.lifeway.com/LivingInTruth*

CALL TO ACTION:

Continue to encourage others by posting any of the following statements to your social media sites or create your own posts. Place a hashtag on keywords like "salvation," "WordofGod," and "authority," if you want more people to see your posts. Tag me if you want to be retweeted or shared! @maryjosharp #LivingInTruth

Christians may lay a foundation of salvation in Jesus Christ, but construct the house of their life upon the shifting ground of worldly culture. #LivingInTruth

Hearing the #WordofGod and acknowledging it as true is different from obeying the Word and constructing your life upon it. #LivingInTruth

The human is the only creation of God made in the image of #God (Gen. 1:27). #LivingInTruth

A Christian can begin to lose confidence in her beliefs, not because she does not have evidence, experience, or trustworthy authority, but due to the idleness of her mind. #LivingInTruth

We can have a reasonable trust in the authority of God. #LivingInTruth @maryjosharp

I find it convicting that the disciples had eyewitness testimony, empirical evidence, physical fact, and yet they could still doubt. #LivingInTruth

Jesus knows that people will still struggle with trusting Him. #LivingInTruth @maryjosharp

The people around you are looking for authenticity, a person who actually trusts in God. #LivingInTruth

We experience difficulty persuading others to trust in God when we ourselves really haven't trusted Him. #LivingInTruth @maryjosharp

Over the years, I've heard a lot of sound bites about conversations, evangelism, and sharing the gospel. From expressions such as "You aren't promised another day [to share the gospel]" to "You may be the only Jesus a person sees" to "How can you say you love Jesus and not share him with a dying world?"

At least in my experience, these sayings swim around in my head leading to a state of confused conviction, so that I end up with more questions. Ironically they leave me with less desire to share my beliefs. I wonder: "Do I not really love Jesus?" or "Do I not really love people?" or "What's wrong with me that I think I have another day to share the gospel?"

While understanding that these sound bites have good intentions, we need move beyond simple catch phrases into the messy world of our thoughts and assumptions. We need to discover what beliefs are really informing our view of conversations about God.

Albert Einstein said, "Anyone who doesn't take truth seriously in small matters cannot be trusted in large ones either."[1]

How would you apply this statement to sharing your beliefs about God with others?

Though Einstein wasn't addressing the issue of sharing beliefs, the general principle in his statement applies to our conversations about God. If people perceive that we are not trustworthy in seeking out the truth in smaller, everyday matters, how will they learn to trust us in issues of great importance, like belief in God? The greatest subject we will ever discuss is on belief in the Savior of the universe. That conversation is inextricably tied to the foundation of our belief in God. So what do you really believe? And how do you know that?

· · · · ·

CONVERSATION GOAL: To establish Jesus as the only trustworthy foundation for your beliefs and your life

What two different kinds of ground did the builders chose in Jesus' parable in Matthew 7:24-28?

During the storm, what happens to the houses built on different ground?

Jesus uses these houses as a metaphor for what teaching?

Jesus paints a picture of two houses built on different types of ground: bedrock and sand. You have to dig deep into the earth to build on bedrock. Sand is easily accessible on the surface.

The house on bedrock can withstand trial because it has a solid base that will not shift in a storm. The house on sand cannot withstand trial because it has an untrustworthy and shifting foundation.

In the parable, the house built on bedrock actually has a foundation laid on that bedrock. Whereas, the house built on sand has no foundation at all. One house was built with an intention of surviving storms and trials. One house was built with no future thinking about the impending storms of life.

The fundamental truth of Jesus' teaching is that you must not only lay a foundation, but also build your entire life—your house—on the only trustworthy ground: the solid bedrock of Jesus Christ and His teachings. Otherwise, your house—your life—will be pulled apart by trials. The trials that come your way will demonstrate the flawed construction.

The Baker New Testament Commentary states, "Both of the men mentioned in this parable are builders, for to live means to build. Every ambition a man cherishes, every thought he conceives, every word he speaks, and every deed he performs is, as it were, a building block. Gradually the structure of his life rises. Not all builders are the same, however. Some are sensible, some foolish."[2]

Some Christians appear to have laid a foundation of salvation in Jesus Christ, but seem to construct the house of their lives upon the shifting ground of worldly culture. Hearing the Word of God and acknowledging it as true is different from obeying the Word and constructing your life upon it.

How would you describe to a new believer the difference between simply believing something is true and building your life on truth?

How would you answer someone who said: "But I have professed Christ as Lord and therefore I have a house built on the trustworthy foundation"?

At the beginning of Jesus' teaching in Matthew 7:24, who exactly has built a house on the trustworthy foundation that is Jesus Christ?

How would you explain the difference between a person who just hears Jesus' teachings and one who puts them into practice?

I am belaboring the point specifically because the teaching is so important. Please clearly answer for yourself: Why is building on—not merely giving lip service to—the trustworthy foundation of Jesus' teachings so essential?

Jesus connects a solid foundation to a life that is carrying out His teachings. Carefully understand something here—Jesus certainly did not teach that we earn God's favor by our efforts. To avoid the error of works-based righteousness, think of His saying as a reality check. In reality, if a house is built on a solid foundation, we can see the effects of the foundation's trustworthiness.

In 2008, our home was hit by Hurricane Ike. The storm tore our roof off in certain areas. Rain flowed into the house damaging the floor, furniture, ceilings, and more. The force of the winds ripped our landscaping out of the ground. Yet, our home was generally intact. Our house had been built on a foundation properly laid to withstand the storms that hit our area. We saw the trustworthiness of the foundation in the testing of its construction by a great trial.

What would you describe as the greatest trial you have had to endure in your lifetime?

What has been the greatest test your foundation of obedience to Christ's teachings has faced?

What was your response to each of the trials? Or to the one event if the same trial represented both?

What false beliefs about God have you seen in the Christian community and outside the Christian world view?

Trials not only test our faith, in the sense of stretching us, but also provide a reality check, to see if our faith is genuine. In difficult situations, we are faced with the question, "On what have I built my life?"

Jesus said that those who have actually trusted Him as the bedrock of their entire lives are those who actually do what He says. So it's not just in trials that we find the answer to the question above. The answer lies in our everyday thoughts and habits.

What results may follow daily living out one or more of those false beliefs?

What are some areas of your life where you still need to build on the foundation of Jesus (even after you've trusted Him for salvation)?

What is informing your thoughts and your habits? Are you centering everything on the bedrock of truth?

When we do not daily build on the foundation of Jesus—when we do not practice His teaching— how do you think that affects our ability to converse with others about God?

This is where Jesus' teaching becomes hard for me. I know that I am not always centering my thoughts and habits on Him. Do I prevail against the trials of my own temptation to wander in thought and practice? That is the difficult question for me.

This week I want us to understand and identify the effects of false beliefs in our daily lives. I'm not sure that Christians today understand that both true and false beliefs have consequences. We must seek Christlikeness with intentionality. We are trying to acknowledge and rid ourselves of as much falsity as possible, so that we will be freed up to follow Christ.

One area for which I did not trust God was the area of conversation with others. I could certainly do an evangelistic push or street witnessing with my church for an allotted time. However, I was not someone who could talk with people anywhere, anytime about God. I harbored conflicting thoughts about whether or not I was "pushing my religion" on people and whether or not my beliefs in God were well-founded.

Even though I had trusted Jesus for eternal life, apparently I didn't trust Him for daily life. To change this, I had to engage in the hard work of identifying what I actually believed about life and the world. I had to begin making my life consistent with the biblical truths I professed to believe. As I actively and intentionally build my daily life upon the foundation of trust in Jesus, I become more confident in conversation about God.

CONFIDENCE BUILDER: For every believer, Jesus Christ is the ultimate, perfect foundation. He is flawless. He is the truth, and relationship with Him is eternal, abundant life. However, what we build on that foundation can contain flaws. For example, I had flaws in my thinking. I was trusting Jesus for salvation, but not in the small things of daily living. I trusted myself more than Jesus. I trusted myself for what to eat, how to dress, how to decorate my home, how to treat my daughter, how to plan my day, how to do my job, how to interact with my husband, how to act at church, how to solve relational problems, how to emotionally respond to situations, etc. All these small areas where I relied on my own thinking and rationale added up to a life built on sand. It's no wonder I had problems with conversing about belief in God, when so much of my life was built on trusting myself.

At the end of the story in Matthew, Jesus says, "And the rain fell, and the floods came, and the winds blew and beat against that house, and it fell, and great was the fall of it" (Matt. 7:27, ESV). Why was the fall so great? Because of the magnificence of the house! Remember, His metaphor is about a human life built on faulty grounding. The human is the only creation of God made in the image of God (Gen. 1:27). Humans were made in a way that they should rule over and care for the rest of creation. When that human life falls due to one's own poor construction, the image of God is distorted and the fall is great indeed.

We have all witnessed Christians who hear the Word of Lord but do not do what He says. According to Jesus such behavior is foolishness (Matt. 7:26). Think of how your thoughts and habits (your life) may be affecting others, for good or for bad, in small ways and in large ways.

As we begin this week, offer a prayer to God for the desire to be transformed by the renewing of your mind. Ask Him to show you where in your life you've built on sand.

DAY TWO

CONVERSATION GOAL: To establish the reason why we recognize Jesus as an authority

Yesterday, we looked at Jesus' story of the houses representing two different grounds for life. I pointed out that you can say you trust Jesus for your salvation (laying a foundation) yet build your life on sand.

I imagine such a person as a dual property owner. After once having laid down a foundation of salvation in Jesus Christ, she proceeds to build her home upon another piece of property where she spends much of her time: the shifting sands of culture. Her daily thoughts and actions construct a huge home in that secular culture neighborhood. ("Shifting Sands Sierra: We don't stand the test of time!") Such a person lives with a divided mind—in other words, a compartmentalized faith.

Today, let's look at how the little things of life demonstrate our bigger view of the world.

When we get up in the morning, most of us have a typical routine. We may brush our teeth, wash our faces, fix our hair and/or makeup, get dressed, eat breakfast, and then head off for the day. Yet what is it that makes us believe that any of these things are necessary as we begin our day? Are we doing these things because that's the way we've always done them? Have we been habituated to do them by watching our parents? Do we have a gene in our DNA or a part of the brain that regulates how we get ready in the morning?

Why would you say you do whatever it is you do in your morning routine?

All of these mentioned activities are seemingly mundane or small things. However, we practice each of them because of some belief we hold to be true. For example, you may brush your teeth because you believe that your teeth will decay if you do not. Where did you get that knowledge? Why do you believe it to be true? You may have read some reports in an article online or in a magazine about health. Maybe your dentist told you. For many of us, we acquired that knowledge from the ritual of our parents dragging us to the dentist.

Which of the following contributed most to convince you to practice the daily habit of brushing your teeth?
❑ You've experienced cavities as a result of not brushing.
❑ Someone you view as an authority figure in this area (dentist, orthodontist) told you.
❑ You read something you believe to be authoritative in this area.
❑ You went to school to get a degree in dental studies.
❑ It's just a habit or ritual you've developed about which you never considered the truth.

How is the daily habit of brushing your teeth a small way of showing a commitment to a larger truth?

Those small commitments—like brushing teeth—demonstrate a commitment to a larger truth concerning human health. They also show an even larger belief that human life is worthwhile, which is why you care for the body. The small things of life demonstrate your larger view of the world—your life philosophy.

How do the small things of life add up to your larger view of the world? These small things are the outworking of what you believe—and what or whom you trust as an authority.

While we usually don't take the time to consider the authority behind our decisions, we build our lives on what we accept as true. Rather than carefully consider truth claims, we just pick up assumptions as we go along in life. That may be OK for dental hygiene but not for making serious life decisions.

I generally need multiple avenues of learning to help me acknowledge any single belief as true. I need to have experience as well as authoritative reading and teaching. But alas, with my limited time on earth I can't get the level of knowledge I want in every area of life. Think of the magnitude of such an endeavor.

If we lack sufficient time and resources to make fully substantiated decisions on all matters, how do you think we can discern truth?

How am I to ever know anything as true—enough to get through even a single day of my life, full of small things in my daily routines? I must trust in authorities, which means I also must be able to discern trustworthy authority.

How did the people respond to Jesus' teaching in John 18:37; Matthew 7:28-29; 13:54; 22:33; 28:18?

According to Matthew 7:28-29, why did the people respond this way?

According to Matthew 28:18, how much authority does Jesus possess?

The Holman New Testament Commentary states, "Unlike the Jewish rabbis and scribes of the time, Jesus did not need to cite other teachers to establish the credibility of His teaching. He spoke out of His own authority. Both the content and manner of Jesus' teaching were overwhelming."[3] As you saw in the Scriptures, Jesus often astounded the people with His teaching. Think about that for a moment. Many of these people, such as the religious leaders, were highly educated. They were not just lowly, unfortunate souls looking for anything to believe. Rather, their amazement came from the depth and truth of Jesus' words and the fact that He spoke out of His own authority concerning the Scriptures, not citing the work of any scholar. He even reinterprets Scripture in His Sermon on the Mount by His own authority!

In addition to amazing, authoritative teaching, what else did Jesus use to establish His authority? (See John 3:2, 6:2.)

Do you believe these are good reasons to trust in Jesus' authority?

Atheists sometimes claim that Christians do not have a trustworthy authority on which to base their lives. This claim can resoundingly strike at the heart of individual Christian's belief in God. A Christian can begin to lose confidence in her beliefs, not because she does not have evidence, experience, or trustworthy authority, but due to the idleness of her mind. She has not analyzed the relation of her beliefs to evidence, experiences, and authority. She may be shaken because she has never thought to ask this question of herself, thus her belief in God appears to be nothing more than a habit or ritual.

Jeffrey: Most Christians don't even want to learn theology, much less what the reasons are for thinking it is true.

MJS: Perhaps you should clarify exactly who most Christians are for me. Do you mean to include the entirety of Christian believers throughout 2000 years of history?

In terms of my earlier illustration, this believer says: "I brush my teeth because that's what I've always done," rather than "I brush my teeth because I have good reason to believe it is true that this practice is good for me."

To have better conversations about our faith, we each need to become the sort of Christian who knows good reasons to trust in God. We need to know this trust can empower and transform us and everyone else. Just like we could never know with 100 percent certainty the reason(s) for everything we think or do in this life (neither could an atheist), we also can never have all the answers about God. However, we can have a reasonable trust in the authority of God.

CONFIDENCE BUILDER: Sometimes when I teach apologetics, a person might say to me that I'm trying to reason my way to God as if human reasoning was sufficient to achieve true, biblical faith. While God gave us reasoning abilities as one way of knowing Him, nevertheless, reason is not fully sufficient to have faith in God—nor is human reason sufficient to explain nearly anything else in our life experience. Thomas Aquinas provides a more well-rounded concept of traditional Christian faith as having three components: 1) *notitia*, or knowledge, 2) *assensus*, or agreement, and 3) *fiducia*, or trust.[4] We have to have some content of knowledge about God before we can believe He exists (Heb. 11:6). We must further agree, i.e., be convicted, that the knowledge is true; it is something we believe is reasonable and responsible (Acts 17:11; 1 Thess. 5:21). We must take the last step of relationally trusting God with our salvation and relying on Him to guide our lives. So our reason plays a role in salvation, but it is only part of the fully orbed understanding of trusting God with all of our lives. Further, we mustn't forget that in a world marred by sin, even our thoughts are corrupted. God seeks after us and draws us to Himself in multiple ways: He can move us emotionally, reveal Himself through visions or dreams, or appeal through the rationality given to us, who have been created in His image.

CONVERSATION GOAL: To learn to trust God with the authority due Him

What reasons to trust Jesus do you see in Matthew 28:16-18? Think both of Jesus' words and the context.

In this passage, Jesus has miraculously risen from the dead and appeared to the disciples, as well as to numerous others. He gives the disciples some final instructions, one final teaching. Why should they believe Him or follow His instructions? Jesus has proved His authority by not only performing miracles for others, but by rising from the grave.

I fear we hear this phrase *risen from the dead* so much that we forget the power of this event and may be missing out on the life-impacting implications. Think of these statements about Jesus and respond to the questions that follow. According to the biblical text, there was a man in history who:

1) gave astounding/astonishing teaching on human nature, the nature of God, and the nature of reality that was ultimately true;
2) could heal people of visible diseases and disorders (leprosy, paralysis, schizophrenia);
3) raised people from the dead;
4) spoke words that healed brokenness of heart and changed lives;
5) forgave evil and sin;
6) not only understood nature, but could command nature;
7) claimed to be the Creator of all things, claimed to be God; and
8) brutally died and then miraculously rose from the dead—and that man predicted He would die and rise from the dead.

Would you have sufficient reason to trust in his authority? If you say "no," what would it take for you to actually trust a person as an authority in this life?

Write your own list of what it takes for you to trust a person as an authority and compare your list to the one about Jesus. Are there any similarities or differences? In your group this week plan to discuss your reasoning for each item on your list.

Do you know anyone who doubts Jesus as an authority? Why does he or she doubt Him? What is his or her list of criteria for establishing someone or something as an authority in his or her life?

If you've never asked someone the questions above, keep them in mind for the next time a person outright rejects Jesus as an authority.

CONFIDENCE BUILDER: Over the years, I have found that atheists will try to discredit, scoff at, or mock a Christian's trust in the authority of Jesus, while at the same time holding numerous beliefs for which they do not have a thoughtful basis or authority. I watched a debate, in which a Christian scholar pointed out that his atheist opponent actually had a lot more blind faith in many things than a Christian. While the atheist denied this, arguing that he made decisions based on a thorough review of the statistics relevant to his situation, the Christian pointed out that there were so many decisions made in a single day, a person could not even get out of bed in the morning if they were to try to review statistics and establish human authorities for everything! Many times, we rely on our culture, traditions, and habits to inform our daily lives without even thinking about it, and this is necessary to normal human functioning. Happily, Christians, by believing in a Creator who knows His own creation and what is best for that creation to thrive, can live consistently within that truth, as opposed to the unlivable standard of a skeptical atheist who must review statistics and consult all the authorities before every move he makes. Christians are completely reasonable to think and act upon the reliable authority of the risen Lord and His Word.

Looking again at the passage from Matthew 28, some of the eleven disciples "doubted" Jesus even after He gave the most convincing possible evidence for His credentials as the ultimate authority by rising from the dead. While commentators are uncertain as to what kind of doubt these disciples harbored, they speculate that the disciples could have been unsure whether or not they should worship Jesus, whether or not they were really seeing the risen Jesus, or if they could trust His authority. In any case, I find it convicting that these disciples had eyewitness testimony, empirical evidence, physical fact, and yet they could still doubt.

Do you find yourself having a difficult time believing Jesus is the ultimate authority in the universe? If so, on what do you rely as an authority instead?

How has that person/text/thing proven it is worthy of your trust in its authority?

VERBAL GIFT CARD:
"I have good reason to trust in the authority of Jesus Christ and His teaching."

When a person does not trust Jesus as an authority, she is shifting the authority to someone or something else, whether or not she is aware of doing so. It is a vital practice to the flourishing Christian life to find the root problem—the foundational flaws—to see what we are actually trusting as the authority for many of our daily thoughts and practices.

To find out what others believe to be their authoritative source is also an extremely effective practice in conversation. When we understand who or what a person trusts as authoritative, we can better minister to them in spite of their currently entrenched habits and thoughts.

You may not struggle with accepting the authority of Jesus, but many people certainly do. Let's look at two passages to help us see why we can trust in the authority of Jesus.

What does Jesus call Himself in John 10:11-15?

What does that title mean?

Jesus contrasts His title with another kind of person. Who is that person? What is the other person's goal?

In John 10:10, Jesus contrasted His life-giving work of death and resurrection to the work of the thief, who only comes to steal life. To recognize Jesus as an authority, we must acknowledge the impacting difference between the two. We trust Jesus with authority because He sacrifices Himself for us. Jesus wants to take the consequence of our sin—death—from us.

The thief, rather, brings death—the consequence of sin—to us. If ever a person was trustworthy of authority, it is the one who gives life by freely taking the consequence of sin, death.

However, Jesus knows that people will still struggle with trusting Him. In John 14, when addressing Philip's request to see the Father, Jesus replies to Philip that the one who has seen Jesus has seen the Father. Yet knowing the hearts of men, He states, "Believe Me that I am in the Father and the Father is in Me. Otherwise, believe because of the works themselves" (John 14:11).

Before you trusted Jesus, what held you back from trusting the One who laid down His life for you?

What elements of your journey of faith coming to trust Jesus could be helpful to those who have not trusted Him?

What can you take from today's lesson on authority to better prepare yourself to "make a defense to anyone who asks you for a reason for the hope that is in you; yet do it with gentleness and respect" (1 Peter 3:15b, ESV)?

FOR FURTHER STUDY

If you need to check out the evidences surrounding Jesus' resurrection as a historical event, you can explore many good works on the subject.

WEBSITES:
- Michael Licona's Risen Jesus Ministries: *www.risenjesus.com*
- Gary Habermas' Official website: *www.garyhabermas.com*
- BeThinking.org articles on the Resurrection: *www.bethinking.org/resurrection*

BOOKS:
- Timothy Keller, *The Reason for God*, Chapter 13, "The Reality of the Resurrection" (New York: Penguin Group., 2008).
- Lee Strobel, *The Case for Easter* (Grand Rapids: Zondervan, 1998).
- Gary Habermas, *The Risen Jesus and Future Hope* (Washington D.C.: Rowman & Littlefield Publishers, 2003).

DAY FOUR

CONVERSATION GOAL: To be trusted in small matters and to also be trusted in big matters such as sharing the gospel of Jesus Christ

2

It may seem odd in an apologetics-based Bible study to spend so much time on personally trusting in the authority of God. Shouldn't we just read and discuss the arguments for God's existence and for Jesus' resurrection and for the Bible as an authoritative text? Think about that question.

If we did go over these arguments right now and came to a point at which you have enough reason to believe each one as true, would you immediately change your thoughts and actions to absolutely conform to biblical truth? Why or why not? Plan to discuss this question with your group this week.

If merely knowing and being convinced of the arguments for the existence of God and validity of Scripture would not be sufficient to motivate us to obey and engage in presenting truth, what do you think would motivate us?

The past 2,000 years of Christianity provides more than enough resources to answer the tough questions of our day. Yet, we still have trouble with conversation about those tough questions or about our beliefs. Something else seems to be in the way. It is not enough to have the answers to the hard questions. We must also put those answers into practice in our lives. That requires surrender to God.

In Matthew 16:24-27, what does it mean to "deny" yourself?

What does it mean to deny yourself in the context of having good conversation about belief in God? Or why must you deny yourself to have a good conversation on hard questions about God?

How good would you say you are at actually denying yourself moment-by-moment?

The answers to hard questions are readily available to us, but we seem to get in the way of spreading the good news. One way we do this is by becoming defensive in conversation. Sometimes, when we hear an aggressive, or just difficult, question or statement, our first instinct is to protect ourselves. (See our next Confidence Builder for some help on this one.)

While we actually face few instances of true persecution, we face more subtle situations that cause us to feel threatened. In our culture we need to overtly resist an overprotective instinct. We need to develop a trust in the authority of Jesus over every part of life. Only such trust will overcome our fears.

The people around you are looking for authenticity, a person who actually trusts in God. They are checking to see if you say one thing, but believe another. Defensiveness or easy agitation does not demonstrate a belief in a God who is the most powerful being of which a person could conceive.

CONFIDENCE BUILDER: When I use the phrase *protect ourselves* I do not wish to simply convey a shy, introverted, or easily rattled person. As humans with many different personalities, protection can come in many forms. We may protect ourselves through a self-centered approach to the discussion, turning the conversation towards only what we want to discuss. We may protect ourselves by being the first one to strike, laying down an aggressive zinger or showing off our knowledge with technical terms. In this way, we perhaps come across as overly confident and arrogant. We may even be the person who desires to just get along with or make peace with others as protection. If we have a protective stance, we will most likely not engage in difficult questions and discussions that make us uncomfortable.

We all do it. What would you say are some of your ways to protect yourself in conversation?

When you get defensive or easily angered what do you think you are communicating or demonstrating about God to the other person in the conversation?

I used to get easily agitated when I was worn out from work. My daughter was usually the target of my anger because she was readily available. She told me one time that she got in trouble for things that didn't seem

to matter. I later discovered that I was portraying an image of God to her that was mired in a lifestyle of suiting my momentary impulses and changing moods. What a poor reflection of God.

I'm certain now that I was showing her I didn't really trust God's authority. You cannot think that by merely communicating the correct words people will magically come around to trusting Jesus. They are looking for a lifestyle that displays trust in God and words that give life. As Billy Graham famously said about the testimony of our lives, "We are the Bibles the world is reading; We are the creeds the world is needing; We are the sermons the world is heeding."[5]

What do you think are some practical behavior changes Jesus meant by, "take up your cross" (Luke 9:23, NLT)?

What does take up your cross mean in the context of having good conversation about belief in God?

We will endure suffering and mockery if we follow Jesus, especially if we wish to share the pure, refining fire of His love that burns the wayward soul with conviction. We must come to understand the difference between the suffering and mockery brought on by a person being painfully convicted by the Holy Spirit, and the suffering and mockery we bring on ourselves when we live with a self-serving attitude.

I have seen the damage of a retort from a non-Christian on a Christian who used apologetics or general conversation to serve their own selfish egos. Consider that in light of what Peter writes in 1 Peter 2:20 (NASB): "For what credit is there if, when you sin and are harshly treated, you endure it with patience? But if when you do what is right and suffer for it you patiently endure it, this finds favor with God."

If we sincerely trust in Jesus and genuinely love people, then we will be able to forgive their mockery and bless them with truth even as we are blessed by God for our patience.

Rate yourself (from 1 to 6) on your trust in Jesus as an authority with everything, big and small, including your everyday conversations.

1 |——————————————————| 6

What do you think you can do to increase your trust in Jesus so that you don't feel as personally threatened?

We saw in Day Three that Jesus is a trustworthy authority on truth. Now we need to take the next step of conforming our thoughts and actions to His authority. I'm not just talking about the "big stuff" like salvation, hot political issues, and major life choices. I'm also talking about trusting Jesus in the small things of everyday life, which accumulate as evidence for trusting in Him for the big things too.

Name some areas where you are doing a pretty good job of trusting Jesus.

Over what things do you think you need to give Jesus greater authority in your life? Are there some things—even very small things—for which you do not necessarily trust Jesus?

Let's take the Einstein quote from the beginning of the week a bit further now. Notice he says that if we cannot be trusted in small matters, we also cannot be trusted in matters that are great. This is true because—as we have seen—the small matters are a daily outworking of what we actually believe. If we can be trusted with little, we can be trusted with much.

In Matthew 25:14-30, what did the master give each servant?

What did the master require of each servant?

What was the master's response to each of the servants?

vv. 20-21

vv. 22-23

vv. 24-28

God entrusts each person with gifts to use in the kingdom here and now. One of the gifts He has given us is the gospel. We are to take our treasure of the gospel and invest it in others. He knows the risks involved in spreading His gift, especially in a world full of humans in which evil is rampant. He still requires us to be trustworthy in what He has given to us to do until His return.

When our Master returns, He will require an account of what we did with what He gave us. In the passage, we saw that the master gave to each person in accordance with their ability. Don't miss that point!

The just master didn't require the same results of every person, nor the same method of investment, but he did require each person to use the gift wisely.

Think of how this parable applies in having conversations with others about belief in God. If you are a person others consider untrustworthy in small matters, then they will not trust you with something as great as the gospel.

How does your everyday life, the small things, demonstrate to others that you are trustworthy with greater things, like the gospel of Jesus Christ?

How do you wisely invest God's gift of the gospel in others?

Has something been holding you back from risking involvement with non-Christians? If so, what?

No matter how we choose to spread the message, and invest our gift of the gospel, the Master is asking us to do so. In the context of our study, we are to spread truth even through the smallest of matters so that we will be trusted in spreading truth in the larger matters. According to *The Holman New Testament Commentary on Matthew*, "Believers also are required to obey Jesus in all things, even when risk is involved, even when we do not see the end results."[6]

CONFIDENCE BUILDER: Being trustworthy in small matters is not the same thing as expecting perfection from yourself. I hope you caught the difference. Trusting God as the authority in all areas of your life should naturally overflow into everything you say and do. However, this overarching idea is to be understood within the context of sanctification, a life that is journeying towards Christlikeness, even if that life journey is still very young. A first step towards trusting God is recognizing where you currently do not trust His authority. The next step is to accept where you are in trusting God and not overly worry whether or not you are at the level you should be. By not beating yourself up, you show that you trust God to complete the good work He has begun in you. The third step is to choose one (or more areas) in which you will make a conscious effort to trust in God's guidance. Remember, this is a lifelong process and one that will only be perfected when we see our Lord face-to-face.

2

CONVERSATION GOAL: To trust the Lord as the actual authority in every area of life, more easily opening up conversations on beliefs

This week's study is a particularly difficult one for me, if I'm honest. Sure, I'll give lip service to the fact that I trust God as an authority in all areas of my life—but do I really believe that statement? If I want to get to the point where I actually believe God is a trustworthy authority in every area of my life, I have to first admit that I'm not currently all the way there. Then I have to desire to trust Him as my authority. I must stop grasping at my own authority and clinging to the authorities of a worldly culture. The problem for me is that sometimes I don't even know when I'm doing so. Further, when a friend corrects me, I can slip into defensiveness, rationalizing my way out rather than seeing God in the moment.

As we close out this week, would you consider making a commitment to consciously trust God with the authority He rightly deserves? Journal your thoughts about this step.

That means you must also trust God with your patterns of thought and your habits. You have to peel back the layers of self-serving traits you've built up over the years and peer at the foundation of your life. Have you actually built your life (including your thoughts) upon the bedrock of Jesus, or is there much you've built upon the sand? Ask yourself the following questions and take the time to write out your thoughts, prayers, or commitments.

1) **Would others consider me trustworthy to deliver the most important message in all of human history? Why or why not?**

2) **Have I turned to other authorities for my life? What are they? In what areas of life am I trusting them?**

3) **How has denying Jesus His rightful authority in some areas of my life potentially hurt my ability to talk with others about my belief in God?**

4) **What is one thing you can do right now with what you've learned this week?**

In my Bible study, *Why Do You Believe That?*, I explain that Christians are not engaging non-Christians in more conversations on faith because the Christians do not know what it is that they believe about God or why they believe it. In this study, I hope you see another reason why we shy away from conversation about God: We have faulty thinking that hinders our confidence to share the truth. Essentially, we are not wholly trusting God as the authority in our lives.

We experience difficulty persuading others to trust in God when we ourselves really haven't trusted Him. We're thwarted by our own contradictory thinking, which results from verbally affirming that God is to be trusted in all things, while in practice only trusting God for some things, but not for others. People can detect this divided mind within us just as my young preteen daughter used to see it in me. It may be unconscious on their part, but at some level they can grasp that something about our actions isn't matching up to what we profess.

In his book, *The Divine Conspiracy*, Dallas Willard explains the difference between trusting Jesus solely for remission of sins—a guilt remover—and trusting the real Person of Jesus: "To trust the real person Jesus is to have confidence in him in every dimension of our real life, to believe he is right about and adequate to everything."[7]

Name some evidence from your life that you think demonstrates your trust in Jesus.

What do you think you need to do to trust Jesus to care for you while you take the risk of investing in others?

An honest look at these questions will hopefully provide you with a glimpse at what may keep you from having conversations with others about your belief in God. You may have a root problem of not trusting Jesus' authority in all areas of life.

When we treat our faith as a Sunday-morning thing, an only-on-special-occasions thing, or an only-for-forgiveness-of-sins thing, we are compartmentalizing our faith. By dividing "that which has to do with church and Jesus" from "that which has to do with daily life," we create a false, unbiblical dichotomy of sacred and secular elements of life.

Of course, daily conversation would fall into the category of "that which has to do with daily life." If you've habituated yourself into trusting your way of thinking and acting in daily matters, you're probably not going to trust God with those things that fall into this category like everyday conversations. Like the third servant in the parable of the talents, you may rationalize to yourself why you didn't risk investment. Yet, as we saw in the story, God wants you to trust Him and to risk the investment, because God's authority truly covers all areas of life, in matters great and small.

VERBAL GIFT CARD: "In our lifestyle of comfort in Western culture, we are too easily lulled to sleep. We fail to live the life of obedient, faith-filled 'risk,' and so we fail to bear kingdom fruit, displeasing our Master."[8]

SCIENCE AND FAITH: TWO ARGUMENTS

The world view of scientism is one of the main problems in our culture today creating the rift between science and faith. "Scientism is the belief that science is all the real knowledge there is."[9]

Mathematician and Christian John Lennox Responds to scientism that: "The mathematical intelligibility of nature is evidence for a rational spirit behind the universe."[10]

What are two of the main arguments concerning the relationship of science and faith in God?

#1. SCIENCE IS THE ONLY WAY TO KNOW TRUTH.

The idea that science is the only way to know truth seems to be gaining quite a bit of traction in the popular realm. World-renown physicist, Stephen Hawking, and nobel prize winner, Harry Kroto, are two of the idea's proponents. Kroto stated in a speech at the 2011 Lindau Nobel Laureate Meeting, "I'm gonna talk about what science is because it's a totally misunderstood sort of subject. There are aspects of science which are important. ... But for me, the most important, by far, is that it's the only philosophical construct we have to determine truth with any degree of reliability."[11]

To address the problematic thinking in Kroto's statement is difficult, not simply because it is logically flawed, but also because it comes from people we trust as intellectuals, from people who should know better. Plus, to say something against these kind of intellectuals in public will earn the average Christian an accusation of stupidity, even if the Christian's assessment is true.

Andrew Brown, a religion writer for The Guardian journal in the United Kingdom, assessed Kroto's comment as follows: "The illogical positivism of Kroto's talk is symptomatic of a widespread problem. Although Kroto is exceptional in his self-confidence and lack of intellectual self-awareness—few other people would state as baldly as he does that science is the only way to establish the truth—no one in the audience seems to have reacted with a healthy giggle. They may have felt there was something a bit off about the idea, but the full absurdity was veiled by layers of deference and convention. The great attraction of telling everyone else to think, to question, and to take nothing for granted is that it makes a very pleasant substitute for doing these things yourself."[12]

Brown is on to something very important: an idea does not become true because someone of great intellect said it. Look back at Kroto's statement. Brown made this assessment, "Think about this for a moment. Is it a scientific statement? No. Can it therefore be relied on as true? No." Brown pointed out that Kroto made a self-refuting statement. No method of science can prove that the methods of science are the only way to know truth. Therefore, Kroto's statement fails to meet its own requirement for knowing truth. By his own standard, his statement about science would prove false.

Further explaining the problem with this statement, Philosopher J.P. Moreland points out, "It is a philosophical statement about science. How could the statement itself be quantified and empirically tested? And if it cannot, by the statement's own standards, it cannot itself be true or rationally held."[13] Moreland proceeds to explain some philosophical views that are necessary presuppositions of science. First, "science must assume that the mind is rational and that the universe is rational in such a way that the mind can know it."[14] Second, science also assumes that the laws of logic are true, that numbers exist, that language has meaning, and that truth exists. Third, science assumes that experiments should be reported honestly and that truth-telling is a moral virtue. None of these presuppositions of the scientific endeavor are provable by any methods of science. Rather, these are all philosophical assumptions that must accepted in order to practice science.[15]

As Christians, it is vital to lovingly point out errors in reasoning such as the one above. If you encounter the statement, "science is the only way to know truth" or a variation thereof, you should ask, "How do you know that?" We are not pitting science against our faith. We believe science is a reasonable endeavor because of our faith in God, but the methods used in science are certainly not the only way to know truth.

#2. SCIENCE IS EVIDENCE-BASED, WHILE RELIGION IS NOT EVIDENCE-BASED.

John Lennox states, "Christian belief has never been about having no evidence: the gospels were written to provide evidence, as the beginning of Luke's gospel attests."[16] The flaw in objection #2 relates to the kind of evidence available. Typically, the scientific method utilizes direct observation and repeatable experimentation to prove a hypothesis. The Christian faith is, in part, based on historical events recorded in multiple texts put together in one body of work: the Bible.

The Christian text is a different kind of evidence called circumstantial evidence. It cannot be repeated or directly observed, but it is a type of evidence utilized in court to determine a person's guilt or innocence. Just as a detective can discern truth about a past event from circumstantial evidence, we too, can discern truth from the biblical texts, if we don't simply reject this kind of evidence a priori. Due to the sensitive nature of religious beliefs, rather than thoughtfully engage and consider, people reject circumstantial evidence for the truth of those beliefs upfront.

Further, many scientists, through their research, believe they have good evidence and arguments that point towards a universe created by God. William Dembski argues the evidence for an Intelligent Designer through the construction and dynamics of living cells. Guillermo Gonzalez argues for the existence of a Creator due to the fine-tuning of the necessary constants of the universe that must exist for life to exist on earth. John Polkinghorne, a physicist at Cambridge University wrote a book titled *Science and the Trinity* in which he argues that the Trinity is exactly the sort of explanation scientists are looking for when they search for a "Theory of Everything." Frank Tipler, one of the world's leading theoretical physicists, argued that the ultimate cause of our universe is Triune—it's "three-in-one." It was only later that he tied this together with Christianity and gave his life to Jesus Christ based on his research in the sciences. It is irresponsible—and most likely denotes a strong confirmation bias—to outright reject these scientists' findings without engaging in rigorous review of their work.[17]

FOR FURTHER INVESTIGATION ON TRUSTING
THE EVIDENCE OF THE GOSPEL TESTIMONIES:
J. Warner Wallace, *Cold-Case Christianity* (Colorado Springs: David C. Cook, 2013).

FOR FURTHER INVESTIGATION ON SCIENCE AND FAITH:
Lee Strobel, *The Case for a Creator* (Grand Rapids: Zondervan, 2004).

William Dembski & Michael Licona, *50 Evidences for God* (Grand Rapids: Baker Books, 2010).

John Lennox, *God's Undertaker: Has Science Buried God?* (Oxford: Lion Hudson, 2006).

J.P. Moreland, *Scaling the Secular City*, Chapter 7, "Science and Christianity" (Grand Rapids: Baker Books, 1987).

Guillermo Gonzalez, *The Privileged Planet* (Washington D.C.: Regnery Publishing, 2004).

Frank Tipler, *The Physics of Christianity* (New York: Doubleday Pub. Group, 2007).

TO EXPLORE FURTHER ON WAYS OF HOW WE KNOW TRUTH:
Mitch Stokes, *A Shot of Faith (to the Head): Be a Confident Believer in an Age of Cranky Atheists* (Nashville: Thomas Nelson, 2012).

3

LISTEN TO DISCOVER TRUTH

GROUP

KEY CONCEPTS THIS WEEK:

1) listening well to others begins with listening well to God

2) recognizing subjectivity versus objectivity in a person's statement can greatly aid in conversations about God

QUESTIONS FOR DISCUSSION:

1) In what ways do you intentionally seek to hear God?

2) How can you get started or better develop in your skills in hearing from God?

3) How does Jesus' authority and our desire to listen to Him relate to each other?

4) Why do you think people have difficulty expressing what they believe is objectively true versus expressing their own subjective opinions on matters about belief in God?

5) Why is learning to identify subjectivity so important to our conversations about God?

6) How can you begin using your knowledge of subjectivity versus objectivity in discussing your beliefs about God?

7) People argue many hot topics in our society from subjectivity. Can you name any? How are these topics argued from subjectivity?

CALL TO ACTION:

Will you help share the truth you are learning in this study? If so, post one of the following statements to any of your social media sites. Tag me if you want to be retweeted or shared! @maryjosharp #LivingInTruth

I care about thinking through issues objectively. #LivingInTruth @maryjosharp

The one who gives an answer before he listens—this is foolishness and disgrace for him. Pv. 18:13 #LivingInTruth @maryjosharp

Who is your Nineveh? God cares and is concerned for them. #LivingInTruth @maryjosharp

Are you actually listening to understand people? #LivingInTruth @maryjosharp

In conversations about belief in God, we need to show respect for the other person in practical and meaningful ways. #LivingInTruth

Godly wisdom results from accepting counsel and instruction from God, and then putting that learning into practice. #LivingInTruth

Paul explicitly states that either Jesus rose from the dead or He did not rise from the dead—an objective claim. #LivingInTruth

In our current society, people struggle with the difference between a subjective and objective statement. #LivingInTruth

DAY ONE

CONVERSATION GOAL: To learn to listen well as an act of obedience to God

Let's begin this week with a project. Pick a subject that typically causes your blood pressure to rise (or at least gets you slightly angry). For our purpose, let's keep the issue to a current hot topic in our society; that will help narrow the scope. The more honest you are about the topic that bothers you, the better this project will be.

Choose your topic and jot it here. Abbreviate or use your own code if you wish.

We are going to learn to listen to people discuss that topic for the purpose of wisely ministering to them in that area of discussion. Each day, beginning today, we'll relate the lesson back to your chosen topic and practice hearing what is actually said. We'll start with a passage from Scripture on why we should be good listeners.

Who is present on either side of Jesus in Matthew 17:1-6?

What three things did God say about Jesus?

What do you think it means to "listen" to Jesus?

Remembering last week's study on establishing authority, we can see here that God places the two men with the most authority in Jewish lives on either side of Jesus. God is visually establishing Jesus' authority. He then verbally establishes Jesus' authority with the three statements, "This is my son," "with whom I am well pleased," and "listen to him." *The Holman New Testament Commentary* reveals that the Greek phrase here means to always listen or to keep on listening to Jesus.[1] The significance of God's command to listen to Jesus in the presence of these two Jewish authorities is that God elevated Jesus' word above all others. Jesus is the ultimate authority to whom we must listen.

In this passage, God commands us to listen to Jesus as an ultimate authority. How have you been doing with that command? How do you regularly take time to "hear" the Word of the Lord?

How would you explain to a new believer what listening to God and hearing His Word entails?

As a listener, how do you think others perceive you?

very good	good	fair	poor

To become good listeners in our community, we must first dedicate ourselves to listening to God. Listening can be a difficult task at times. We live in an age with many things to distract us away from studying the Word, receiving preaching and teaching, engaging in conversation with other Christians, allowing silence and solitude (so God can speak and minister to us). As we become a more distracted people, we also become a less focused people, especially with regards to hearing others, let alone hearing God. Yet, even though we have so many distractions, I find that people still evaluate themselves as fairly good listeners.

There's the problem, huh? I'm going to assume that most of us want to be good listeners, especially when it comes to hearing the Word of God. However, we face the obstacle of our own overconfidence in our listening skills. In Tim Muelhoff's book, *I Beg to Differ*, he cites a study on listening skills in the workplace from the *Journal of Business Management*. The managers all ranked themselves in the "good" to "very good" categories for listening skills. Their workers ranked these same managers in the "weak" category.[2]

Over the years I have found that Christians, when asked, are generally quick to say they are fairly good listeners. Yet, when I speak with atheists, especially those who grew up in a Christian home or in church, they express the opposite view. As one said, "I never really felt like Christians were listening to me."

Since God commands us to become those who listen well—first to Jesus—we won't get very far in a conversation on truth if we cannot first be truthful with ourselves about our own ability to listen.

When someone tells you they are not a believer in Jesus Christ, what is your first reaction?

Do you want to truly discover why they do not believe in Jesus? Or are you too impatient to talk about what you know to really listen?

Why do you think you react that way?

Today's social media-driven society feeds off instant gratification and short quips rather than thoughtful, attentive dialogue. Real understanding requires the patience to carefully listen without planning your next comeback.

How can listening be a great service to the person who doesn't believe in Jesus?

If we are not the kind of people who obediently listen to Jesus' teachings, we are probably not going to be the best listeners in other areas. Listening takes obedience, whether it is to the Word of God, to our boss at work, or to our own friends and family. The word *obey* is closely related to its synonym *mind* (as in "mind your manners" or "mind your step").

Whereas, people sometimes have adverse reactions to *obey*, they typically don't have similar issues with the word *mind*. Why? The word *mind* implies that we are thinking about an issue in order to take heed. It implies thoughtfulness on a matter. However, we seem to interpret *obey* as something like mindlessness—to obey like a mind-numbed robot.

This is hugely problematic for our obedience to the Lord. When we obey God, it is not mindlessness, but a thoughtful consideration to take heed because He has the proper authority to give commands. When God commands us to listen to His Son, it is with good reason.

What does Proverbs 19:27 say happens when we stop listening to the Lord?

How does straying from the words of knowledge impact our ability to listen to others?

Now let's take your project into account. Today, let's end with a prayer that you will learn to listen to God when it comes to handling your particular issue. At this point, you are not going to look up multiple arguments to support your side. Instead, you are going to try to understand the people behind your hot topic issue and recognize that God knows the intentions of their hearts. So your goal today is to love the people God loves who hold to the view on the other side of the issue.

Write your hot topic:

What attitude do you think Jesus would use in approaching the people who hold the opposing view of this topic?

Write a prayer as if God has called you to lead them through this tough issue.

Can you identify any example in Scripture of Jesus correcting a person who is gravely mistaken on an issue or situation? If so, describe the situation.

How can you model His approach in your life?

One thing that helps me when I'm discussing difficult issues with people who adamantly oppose my view is to remember a statement by the commander of the Lord's army when Joshua asked him, "Are You for us or for our enemies?" (Josh. 5:13). The commander replied, "Neither." How often I forget to avoid an "us" versus "them" mentality when listening to opposing viewpoints.

The Lord wishes for all mankind to be saved (2 Pet. 3:9; 1 Tim. 2:4). As we listen to others and prepare ourselves to engage in ministering in truth and love, we must always remember that we are in this life together. Further, Joshua's response to the commander was to bow to the ground in reverent worship, and ask, "What does my Lord want to say to his servant?" (Josh. 5:14). As you begin to engage people with opposing views, keep this scene in mind and ask yourself, "What does my Lord want to say to His servant?" We can learn in every situation.

CONFIDENCE BUILDER: Remember Nineveh? God sent the prophet Jonah to call Nineveh to repentance. Jonah was to preach salvation found in God. However, Jonah was sickened by the people's views and practices. He struggled greatly with his bias towards them. He felt they did not deserve God's salvation. He did not truly wish to see them repent. Do you have a Nineveh? Is it the people who support same-sex marriage or abortion? Is it a people of a different religion or political view? Do you find yourself struggling with your call to minister to these people? If so, remember that Nineveh was involved with all sorts of life-destroying practices, and yet God called them to repentance through Jonah's preaching. As *An Introduction to the Old Testament* states, "Nineveh was a 'vicious and cruel imperial power that constantly threatened his homeland. Jonah felt Israel deserved better than to have its God forgive its enemies."[3] In response to Jonah's attitude, the Lord said, "Should I not have concern for the great city Nineveh?" Through the story, we see God is not just God of those who believe/think/dress/behave just like me, but He is God of the universe. The story of Nineveh is a great reminder to us today to minister to others in a culture that continues to become more polarized and aggressive in handling difficult issues.[4] As you consider your hot topic, it is so important to consider that these views are held by people God loves. He desires that they come into a saving relationship with Him.

POSITIVE EXAMPLE:

MJS: Training in apologetics should be a regular part of discipleship.
—J.P. Moreland

K: @MaryJoSharp you shouldn't have to train believers to defend their own beliefs. That should be easy if you really have the truth...

MJS: @K What do you mean by that?

NEGATIVE EXAMPLE:

K: no thx. Interpretation of the bible is just another way for Christians to cherry pick & bend the message to benefit them.

S: @K Ok is the dictionary ok? In 1828 the dictionary defined a unicorn as any animal with a single horn.

K: @S sounds good.

S: @K what's said is you only regurgitate commonly known sound bites without researching anything. Study. Do your homework. Make GA proud.

K: @S you don't know anything about me. Nice try with the personal insults.

DAY TWO

CONVERSATION GOAL: To learn basic steps towards how to listen well

My husband Roger has served as a church minister of youth and/or worship for over 18 years. He frequently has to handle emotionally difficult situations between church members. In one meeting, he presented a case for the church to make a large purchase. When he finished, a man began adamantly disagreeing with what Roger had said. Roger realized this man had heard the words he spoke yet hadn't really listened to what Roger said. By comparing the man's statement with Roger's initial remarks, Roger was able to show that they didn't disagree at all. So you see, one problem we encounter in conversation is that we give people a turn to talk, but we're actually not paying that much attention to what they say. Worse yet, we may not care what people have to say, an even graver problem.

Today, we'll work on listening well, since the conversations we hope to have could entail some heated topics and discussions.

For what does Proverbs 19:20 say we are to listen?

What is the purpose of listening for this?

The beginning of learning how to listen is to learn what to listen for. As the great teacher in Proverbs describes, you are listening for counsel and instruction so that you will be wise. Wisdom here is not referencing a secular view of intelligence, e.g., IQ score or exam grades. Rather, this godly wisdom results from accepting counsel and instruction from God, and then putting that learning into practice.

Why do you think we must first learn to listen to instruction and counsel ourselves before we can have good conversations with others?

What results have you seen from conversations in which the people involved displayed an obvious lack of wisdom in handling the dialog?

I've been greatly embarrassed and saddened when I've seen Christians resort to attack tactics to get their point across to an atheist or Muslim, or even another Christian believer. My attention was recently caught by an article an atheist wrote called, "Apologetics isn't for the lost, it's for the saved."[5] In it, the author opined that apologists were narcissists who had to be in control of the conversation at all times. Apparently, his experience with "apologists" led him to think that "controlling the conversation" was what apologetics teaches! Of course, we take this one article with a grain of salt, but it probably contains a kernel of truth.

In conversations about belief in God, we need to show respect for the other person in practical and meaningful ways. One of these ways is to actually listen for the other person's point-of-view and/or argument.

What does 1 Thessalonians 5:21 tell us to do in accordance with Paul's teaching?

One reason people are so confused about what is true in our society is that they aren't listening to hear what is actually being argued. We are supposed to be people who test everything so that we can hold onto what is good. This doesn't mean we engage in immoral activities or expose ourselves to everything. Rather, it means that we are supposed to analyze the things we see and hear to know whether or not this is something good.

We discern good and evil using wisdom. So let's look at some practical steps for how to engage in appropriate listening.

#1. Check your motive for the conversation. If you are just in a dialog to prove you are right or to buttress your own ego, you have the wrong motives. Most likely, the conversation will not go well (even if you think it did go well, the other person can pick up on wrong motives; people are perceptive). We listen as part of loving and respecting a human being made in the image of God.

#2. Provide an opportunity for the other person to aptly explain their argument or view, without interruption. This can be so hard—many of us have bad habits in this area, or don't even realize we're doing so. (Remember the study Muelhoff cited.)

#3. Engage in clarifying questions to better understand a person's position. (Next week will help with this area.)

#4. If necessary, repeat their statements back to them. Words and phrases can take on different shades of meaning in our heads. It is helpful to verbalize what you think was said. "Let me see if I understand what you are saying …"

#5. Be aware of your body language and its effect in the specific cultural situation when talking with people. For example, in most Western societies, the ability to look someone in the eye is routinely associated with positive qualities such as confidence, a clear conscience, and respectful attentiveness. Conversely, crossed arms and looking away are attributed to uneasiness, defensiveness, or hiding something.

#6. While listening, find anything on which you can agree. This practice is conducive to a productive conversation for it shows charitable judgment.[6] For example, in past conversations, I've said to atheists who have an erroneous view of the Christian God, "I don't believe in the god you just described either! So I agree with you." My example has an element of humor, but if you can find anything with which to agree, this practice helps the other person open up and trust you with a dialog. A better example might be, "I see that we both care adamantly about our beliefs …"

Now let's look at how these steps can be used in our hot topic project. Which one (or more) of the above steps is going to be most difficult for you with regard to your topic?

Walk yourself through an imaginary conversation on your hot topic. You may even wish to write out the conversation. Think of a statement you've heard recently on your hot topic in opposition to your view. Imagine yourself in a discussion on that statement and how you would normally react. Now visualize how you want to react to produce an atmosphere conducive to dialog. Choose one of the steps above to commit to prayer. Ask God for guidance—as well as comfort—as you seek to improve in listening to an argument.

For more on the nature and purpose of listening to minister, see my study, *Why Do You Believe That? A Faith Conversation.*

CONVERSATION GOAL: To learn to listen for objective versus subjective statements

I recently read an article about a young woman the federal police are tracking. The woman is traveling across America to prominent national forest parks. She hikes into these parks to enjoy their natural beauty—like many people—but she brings in acrylic paint and paints permanent images in a conspicuous location within these parks (generally on boulders and rocks). Many people are incensed by her artwork, calling it vandalism that defaces prized national parks: a federal offense. She argues, "It's art, not vandalism. I am an artist."[7] Further complicating the discussion is an article from *Cosmopolitan* magazine, a highly influential women's magazine, calling the young woman a "hero" for her graffiti artwork. The author at *Cosmo* deemed the woman's actions as positive, inspiring other young women to break some rules.[8]

So, we have an opportunity here to "listen in" on a heated topic with differing views. Let's pretend that

you have two friends who line up on different sides of the debate: Is the woman a vandal or not a vandal? They begin to argue with each and finally turn to you asking, "Well, what do you think?" Before you reply to your friends, let's think through the situation.

Attempt to describe the woman's view.

Now describe the view of those who oppose her.

In your opinion, who has the truth on this matter?

How do you know that?

The graffiti artist made a case that her artwork is not vandalism on the basis of her belief that it is indeed art. The people on the other side of the argument call her artwork a clear case of vandalism on the basis of her chosen canvas, the protected national parks. While it may seem like a cut and dry case due to American laws, notice the *Cosmopolitan* magazine author agreed with the graffiti artist and called her a "hero."

What we need is a standard by which we can judge the truth between the different opinions. However, before we even get that far, we need to learn an important difference that causes us trouble in discerning the truth of situations such as the national park graffiti artist: the difference between subjectivity and objectivity. Not only will this difference help us rightly judge in the national park matter, but knowing the difference will help us in conversations about God. Let's learn two terms we can use in listening to the issues in our culture.

CONFIDENCE BUILDER: If your response to the national park case included something like, "No matter what the woman believes, it's against the law in America to vandalize public or federal property, so that's how I know it is true that she's a vandal," remember man-made laws don't necessarily represent truth about reality. A law is an agreed upon restraint within a community of people. An example where man-made laws do not necessarily match reality would be the law resultant from Roe vs. Wade in which "human" was redefined to exclude an unborn child, thereby changing the status of killing an unborn child from murder to not murder under American law. If it is objectively true that killing an unborn child is murder, then the law would no longer match reality. (Please note: The Roe vs. Wade example is used to discuss *general laws*, not *special cases* such as circumstances where a choice has to be made between the life of the mother and the life of the child.) Another example of man-made laws that did not match reality is the Jim Crow laws that redefined "equality" as "separate but equal" for African-Americans. If it is true that all mankind is equally made in the image of God, then these laws failed to reflect the reality of that equality.

Subjective statement

A *subjective statement* is a statement that is about the subject (the person), but is not necessarily about the object it references. Subjective statements can be true for one person and false for another person. For example, I may say, "*Doctor Who* is the best television series of all time." This statement may be true for me, but it is going to be false for others.

From my statement, do you actually know anything about the show?

Rather, do you now know something about me? What do you know about me?

Can you think of how a subjective statement can be true for one person but false for another person? Be prepared to discuss this question with your group.

When I say, "*Doctor Who* is the best television series," I'm leaving out an important phrase: "In my opinion" or "I think." When I leave these off the front end of my statement, the listener may fail to correctly infer that my statement is about me and about my preferences. My statement almost sounds as if it is about the show. However, I haven't really said anything about the show. I used the show in reference to myself.

Another example of a subjective statement would be, "Chocolate ice cream is better than vanilla." This statement is actually, "In my opinion, chocolate ice cream is better than vanilla," which again is a statement about me, not about the ice cream.

What does a subjective statement tell you?

What does it specifically not tell you?

Objective Statement

An *objective statement* is a statement that is about the object, not about the subject's personal opinions or preference. The statement is either true or false—whether or not I believe it, agree with it, or even know it. For example, I may say, "*Doctor Who* is a British television series." This statement is true for everyone, in all places and all times and is true whether or not an individual even knows that the show exists.

From my statement, what do you know about the show?

Do you know anything about my preferences from the statement?

Though you might assume that I watch or enjoy *Doctor Who* from my statement, you actually have no reason to think so. I did not reference myself in the statement. I'm only discussing the object, which is the show. I'm actually saying something about the show, that it is a British television series. Another example of an objective statement is "The ice cream in the bowl is chocolate." The statement makes no reference

to me. I stated something true for all people—that the ice cream in a particular bowl is chocolate.

In your own words, describe a subjective statement:

In your own words, describe an objective statement:

Why do you think knowing the difference between these two kinds of statements is important when you are listening to others?

A subjective statement can be true for one person and false for another person. An objective statement is either true or false about an object, but it cannot be both true and false. For example, it cannot be true for some people and false for some people that "the ice cream in the bowl is chocolate." This kind of statement is either true or false. To say it is both would be absurd.

In conversation about God, we can get tangled up in discussing subjective statements, which can be true for one person and false for another. It is vital to recognize subjectivity, acknowledge it, and move the conversation over to discussing objective statements, if possible. Why? Let's answer using our example above slightly adjusted to discuss belief in God. Suppose you are listening to your friend and he says, "Christianity is the worst religion."

Is this a subjective or an objective statement?

How can you tell which one it is?

Rewrite the sentence to reflect what you know just based on the statement itself:

If you were to carry on a conversation from this statement without addressing its subjectivity (or even hearing the subjectivity), you wouldn't be very productive or effective. The person making the statement referenced herself and her preference: to her Christianity is the worst religion. To another person Christianity might be the best religion.

Now what would you do? At this point in the conversation, it seems like Christianity is all about personal preferences. So let's say that you remember that this kind of statement says nothing about Christianity (the object) and only references the opinion of the person making the statement (the subject).

What could you say in response to a person making the claim, "Christianity is the worst religion"? Think how you might lower the temperature of the argument rather than add to it.

The response to a subjective statement can be very tricky because it can hurt a person's feelings, since she is actually discussing her own opinion or preference (discussing herself rather than the object). We don't want a person to become defensive and begin protecting her defensive emotion. We want to free her up to consider something objective about Christianity. So here's where we come around to listening again.

Write a question that would give the person an opportunity to move from the subjective statement to an objective statement about Christianity (if you didn't already do so above):

Be prepared to share these questions with your group.

VERBAL GIFT CARD: "I care about thinking through issues objectively. To have fruitful dialogue, I must take care that I'm not just defending a personal preference, but rather an objective truth."

You might try some different questions in an attempt to uncover the problematic subjectivity. For example, you might say, "Help me to understand you correctly. Are you saying that, in your opinion, Christianity is the worst religion? Or are you saying something like it is a provable fact that Christianity is the worst religion?"

At first, your question may confuse her. Our culture has become so individualistic that we may see our subjective statements as objective statements. In other words, we may think our preferences are one-and-the-same with objective truths about the universe. If a person doesn't prefer that God exists, she may equate the truth of her subjective preference (it is true that she prefers God doesn't exist) with an objective truth statement (that God exists or that God does not exist). Currently, separating out the two kinds of statements in the minds of people is very difficult. You may have to explain the difference. The important thing is that you do explain the difference. One of the reasons we have so much trouble discussing our beliefs is that our society is prone to see all beliefs as subjective to individuals. So one of your roles as a believer in the Truth is to help others understand their own statements.

We've addressed some concepts today on which we need to marinate for a couple more days. We'll look at these ideas again tomorrow, but in the mean time let's wrap up our judgment on the national park situation. The woman's defense was that her work wasn't vandalism, it was art.

Is her statement: ❏ subjective or ❏ objective? (don't peek ahead)

This is a particularly tough one because the woman didn't include a statement such as "in my opinion" or "it is my preference" or "it is a known fact" or "objectively speaking." We need to ask her at least one clarifying question to figure out if she thinks she's saying something subjective or objective.

What could you ask the woman to determine if she's saying something subjective or objective?

I might ask her, "Do you mean to say that it is only art and not vandalism based on your own opinion or are you arguing that you can prove that your work is art and not vandalism by offering some kind of evidence for your belief?" So far, the woman has not given us a reasoned case or any kind of evidence that her belief matches reality. Therefore, we are most likely dealing with a subjective statement about her graffiti work. In her opinion, it is art, but not vandalism. Going back to our pretend heated conversation on this issue, how would you respond to your friends who asked, "What do you think?"

Remember our goal is to be able to converse with people on difficult topics in our culture. In order to do so, we must sometimes point out the problem of subjectivity versus objectivity. The young woman seems to have an objective truth problem. She seems to believe that her opinion should be true for all people, in all places, at all times. She seems to think her preferences constitute objective truth rather than a subjective truth.

You will encounter this same issue in discussing belief in God with others in our culture. Some people will believe their opinions and preferences are objective truths. Some people will become easily offended when you discuss belief in God because they cannot separate the subjective from the objective (think of the current mantra of "hate speech") or because a person may view all religious truths as completely subjective. Further, it can be difficult at times for both persons involved in a conversation to discern the subjective versus the objective statements. So we will spend another day learning to listen to discover this particular problem, how to hear it, and what to do.

DAY FOUR

CONVERSATION GOAL: To listen to statements about hot topics to determine subjectivity versus objectivity

We learned yesterday to listen for subjective statements versus objective statements. Today we're going to use your hot topic to better understand statements that are about the person speaking (the subject) and the thing or issue referenced (the object).

Write your hot topic here:

Write a sentence about your topic that is a subjective statement.

Write a sentence about your topic that is an objective statement.

How did you do? If your response is "great" then here's a long-distance high-five! If your response is "not so great," don't worry. We are discussing a difficult problem to understand and to master. It may take some time to grasp, but don't give up. One of the main reasons we have trouble defending what we believe with people who disagree is that we cannot tell the difference between subjective statements and objective statements. Let's do some more practice.

Beside each of the following sentences write "S" for subjective or "O" for objective.

___ Babies need food to grow.

___ Roses are the best flower to give to your wife.

___ The most beautiful color is green.

___ Jesus is God.

I've used these statements in training sessions on truth with churches. Nearly every time, the audience agree on the answers to the first three: objective, subjective, subjective. However, usually people disagree on the last one.

Why does the last statement stimulate disagreement? Is the sentence unclear? No. Does the statement contain negatively charged wording? No. The subjectivity/objectivity of this statement has become hard to discern because it is a hot topic in our culture.

When I say, "Jesus is God" have I said something about myself or about Jesus?

When people get heated about discussing hot topics, they may have unconsciously classified statements like the objective statement above as a subjective statement. They may think the statement I am making is just about my personal preference, much like stating my favorite color. Further, if I do not understand what I am saying—something subjective versus something objective—the conversation can become quickly convoluted. Yet, the intention of my statement is to say something about Jesus, not about myself. This statement is either true or false because it is an objective statement about Jesus.

Why can't the statement "Jesus is God" be both true and false at the same time?

When you say, "Jesus is God," you make a specific claim about Jesus' identity. You claim He is God (divine). This claim either matches the way the world really is (remember our definition of truth from Week One) or it does not match the way the world really is. No other option exists: this claim is true or false. Three laws of logic back us up on this matter.

- The Law of Identity: a thing is what a thing is.
- The Law of Non-Contradiction: a thing is not what it is not.
- The Law of the Excluded Middle: a thing either is or is not.

Let's look at our claim according to each law:

- The Law of Identity: Jesus is God (this is our original claim).
- The Law of Non-Contradiction: Jesus is not non-God (if our original claim is true).
- The Law of the Excluded Middle: Jesus is either God or not God (there is no other logical option; either the statement matches reality or it does not).

Here's another way to think on this issue: If "Jesus is God" can be true for me and false for someone else, then we open up the possibility that Jesus is whatever anyone prefers Him to be because we made it a subjective claim. Therefore, Jesus can be:

1) God
2) Just a prophet
3) One of many gods
4) A myth
5) A good teacher

But according to the laws of logic, to say that Jesus is all of the above is illogical. It is absurd. Now the difficulty for our conversations lies in two parts: 1) hearing the difference between subjectivity and objectivity, and 2) showing a person that difference of belief does not mean we are all making subjective statements about our beliefs.

Read 1 Corinthians 15:12-20. What did the apostle Paul claim in verse 14?

What does he imply in verse 19?

Why is it important that Paul's statement is objective and not subjective?

In this passage the apostle Paul directly refutes the idea that religion is subjective to the individual. He explicitly states that either Jesus rose from the dead or He did not rise from the dead. This is an objective statement that cannot be true for one person and false for another. It is either true or false for all people.

Our society is very confused on this point. We live in a time when people think Paul's statement can be true for one person and false for another. Yet, this way of thinking leads to absurdity.

You may find it difficult to talk with people about belief in God or other hot topics because people have difficulty thinking through things objectively. Many hot issues are placed entirely into the realm of subjectivity. So when people talk to you about their beliefs, they may really be defending their own personal feelings and desires about these topics.

Can you think of any difficulties that could arise in discussing heated topics if people are really only defending their personal feelings and desires?

The difficulty that I have found is that we could never find actual truth—something that is true apart from how we may feel about a thing—if we are only concerned with defending our feelings and desires. Yet, our current society finds it difficult to consider an issue apart from its direct emotional/personal impact on their individual lives. I see more and more people arguing for same-sex marriage, abortion rights, euthanasia, legalization of recreational marijuana, and atheism from the direct appeal to themselves and their feelings, rather than whether something is objectively true about these issues. It is difficult to discern a person's thoughts, but listening to discover how a person is arguing will make a big impact on how you minister to them through conversation. It can also help you avoid making the same mistake of arguing out of personal preferences and desires.

CONFIDENCE BUILDER: Subjectivity vs. Objectivity in Worship Music. My husband has been my worship pastor for more than a decade. Over the years, we've noticed a particular problem with church members commenting on the music in the church. Typically, Roger would get comments such as, "I don't like that song;" "That is an awful song;" or "I don't like that type of music;" and variations thereof. What is problematic is that though we believe these church members would like to see a real change based on their comments, these are subjective statements.

Subjective statements can be true and false at the same time. So one church member may say to Roger, "That was the worst worship set ever," and the statement is true for this church member. Another church member may come along in the same day and say, "That was the best worship set ever," which makes the first church member's statement false for this church member. So now we have a problem: Whose subjective statement do we use as true? Next time you want to give your music minister a statement about the music, see if there is anything objectively true that you can say! It may be a lot more difficult to comment on the music than you originally thought. I've adopted a saying about sharing my likes and dislikes with music ministers, "If you can't say anything subjective that's nice, don't say anything subjective at all."

William: The fact that you believe your variety of truth is of the objective variety is still your subjective opinion.

Roger: Can you clarify for me if this statement belongs to the objective variety of truth or if it is a subjective opinion?

DAY FIVE

CONVERSATION GOAL: To use listening skills to hear the arguments for your hot topic

Let's look back at what we've covered this week. Name one thing you learned from each day this week:

Day One:

Day Two:

Day Three:

Day Four:

Which one of these things had the most impact on you? Was there anything that was particularly difficult to understand or apply? If so, why?

You may have found several answers to that last question. In teaching college students, I have found that learning to hear the difference between subjectivity and objectivity is one of the hardest things the students face. They do not understand how to express an argument on a hot topic in a way that is actually about the topic and not about their view of the topic.

Now, we're going to revisit your hot topic. For this next part, you need to determine your current level of comfort in listening to the opposing view to your hot topic. Are you able to listen, one-on-one, to that friend or family member who adamantly holds to a different view on your hot topic? If yes, you're going to enlist them for today's activity. If no, you'll need to find an article, a news report, or a lecture that takes the opposing view to your position.

While you listen to the person or read the article, pay close attention to how the arguments are stated. Answer the questions below:

1) Is the person/author using subjective or objective statements about the topic?

2) What are some questions you could ask to discover any subjectivity?

3) Are you actively listening to this person with the express purpose of understanding his or her point-of-view?

4) Are you getting defensive? (Has your heart rate increased?)

5) Did you find yourself wanting to stop listening before the presenter/author was finished making his or her case?

If you found yourself answering, "yes," to number five, don't come down on yourself about it. Remember that learning to listen well can be, for some, a life-long learning process. I'm pretty sure it will be for me!

Many times, instead of listening to understand with the purpose of discovering truth and growing in maturity, I am defending my own biases and comfort zone. However, when I go back to the Scriptures from Day One, Matthew 17 and Proverbs 19, they remind me that listening is an act of obedience. Good listening begins with listening to God's Son and trusting in His authority. I can trust Jesus' authority and spend time listening to Him so that I will have the strength—and stomach—to listen to men through the power of the Holy Spirit.

THERE'S A LOT OF DIFFERENCE BETWEEN LISTENING AND HEARING.[9]
— G.K. CHESTERTON

THE OBJECTION OF EVIL

Christian philosopher, William Lane Craig, has noted that the problem of evil certainly presents one of the greatest obstacles to belief in the existence of God. "When I ponder both the extent and depth of suffering in the world, whether due to man's inhumanity to man or to natural disasters, then I must confess that I find it hard to believe that God exists. No doubt many of you have felt the same way. Perhaps we should all become atheists."[10]

The problem of evil is a philosophical objection to the existence of God commonly stated: If God is all-good, all-wise, all-loving, all-just, and all-powerful, why is evil in the world? Or more personally stated versions such as: How can I believe God is good when my son died of leukemia?

The impact of the problem of evil extends to everyone because everyone experiences pain, suffering, and acts of evil. One impacting way we can help others with the objection is to help in understanding what we mean by evil.

The basis of the objection is that evil is real—it has some form of existence. For us to understand what is evil, we must know what is good. For objective evil to exist, objective good must exist as well. We must have a standard of goodness, something that is always good, by which we can judge something as not good, or evil. Let's illustrate this idea. When we say, "She died too young," we are inferring a standard about the length of a person's life. We mean to say that one length of life is good and another length of life is not good. Yet to do so we must have some idea of what is good to recognize that something is not good.

Further, evil is not a thing-in-itself; it has no substance of its own. Evil is the corruption of a good thing. Saint Augustine asserts, "There can be no evil where there is no good."[11] He points out that evil is, in some sense, parasitically related to a standard of goodness. While a person or event may be really evil, that evil could not have existed without some prior or original good. Physical corruption represents the mutilation of things. Moral corruption describes an injustice committed against another.

So to define evil we must find a standard of goodness. Most frequently, I encounter arguments that assume a standard of goodness without giving the source of that standard. For the Christian, God's nature provides us the standard of goodness. Christian philosopher, Douglas Groothius explains, "Biblical theism claims God as the source of all goodness on the basis of both God's character and God's will ... Objective moral values have their source in the eternal character, nature and substance of a loving, just and self-sufficient God. Just as God does not create himself, so he does not create moral values, which are eternally constituent of his being."[12]

But let's go further: What God made was good. God, being perfectly good, made a perfectly good creation (Gen. 1:26, 31; 1 Tim. 4:4). Part of that good creation is freedom, free will. Groothius explains that man is naturally good (accordance with God's creation) but is historically and presently fallen, sinful, and depraved. Man has used his good gift of free will to do very bad things. Evil is a corruption of a good thing.

The discontinuity between man's original creation and his fallen status gives hope for a recovery. It means that an original goodness to mankind has been corrupted. Since man has not always been this way, he does not have to remain this way. Our defects are not hardwired and inescapable. However, it is important to note the contrast here between Christianity and atheistic naturalism. According to atheist biologist, Richard Dawkins, we are indeed hardwired and simply "dancing to the music of our DNA."[13] I explain this quote to my audiences, "Therefore, the singer sings and the painter paints, but also the murder murders and the rapist rapes."

However, notice in the Christian world view, death is not God's original intent for His creation. Death is not good; it is an evil. Notice too that death angers (outrages) Jesus as well as brings Him sorrow (John 11:33,35). We can see that this is not the way things are supposed to be and it matches with our own experience of life and death: death is an enemy.

Death is the consequence of evil. "The wages of sin is death" (Rom. 6:23). While I don't know the physics, chemistry, or biology of how evil brings destruction and death, evil is a corruption of the goodness of creation. We can point to the psychological impact on the physical such as how worry, stress, and depression can make a person physically ill. So though I don't actually know the science of it, I see its effects.

What does God do? Does He just let things be? No, He provides hope for mankind. God defeats evil. He defeats the consequence of the corruption of life (death).

The way God does this is to step into the experience Himself. "He enters our world, lives as a poor man and suffers the full consequences of evil and pain."[14]

The ultimate defeat of evil is the victory over death found in Jesus' resurrection. The historical nature of the resurrection shows us that:

- Evil is a real enemy; it is real.
- Evil is not the way things are supposed to be.
- The corruption of life, the evil that is death, has been answered by God through Jesus Christ (1 Cor. 15:26—the last enemy to be put down is death).

The resurrection of Jesus is the example of the redemption of God's good creation that will take place for everyone (1 Cor. 15:20). As Jesus stated, "I am the resurrection and the life. The one who believes in Me, even if he dies, will live" (John 11:25). The death and resurrection of Jesus also give us an explanation for the reality and source of goodness and evil.

"So paradoxically, even though the problem of evil is the greatest objection to the existence of God, at the end of the day God is the only solution to the problem of evil. If God does not exist, then we are lost without hope in a life filled with gratuitous and unredeemed suffering. God is the final answer to the problem of evil, for He redeems us from evil and takes us into the everlasting joy of an incommensurable good, fellowship with Himself."[15]

4

QUESTION CULTURAL VIEWS & INDIVIDUAL BELIEFS

GROUP

KEY CONCEPTS THIS WEEK:

1) the importance of using questions in conversation

2) clarifying questions in conversations about God

3) analyzing three objections in the areas of science, goodness, and intolerance

QUESTIONS FOR DISCUSSION:

1) How can questions defuse a tense situation?

2) Why do you think Jesus asked questions at times instead of simply giving a teaching or correction?

3) What are some basic questions you can use to clarify a person's beliefs?

4) Why is it important to find out why a person believes something to be true?

5) To have meaningful and productive conversations with people, why do we need to understand the influences that have shaped them?

6) How can you question the idea that science is the only way to know truth?

7) How can you question the idea that we don't need God to be good?

8) How can you question the idea that a standard of goodness is found apart from God?

9) How can you question and respond to the idea that Christians are intolerant?

CALL TO ACTION:

Post the following to any of your social media sites. Place a hashtag on keywords like "science," "good," and "tolerance," if you want more people to see your posts. Tag me if you want it retweeted or shared! @maryjosharp #LivingInTruth

I am a resolute supporter of gaining knowledge and truth through the methods of #science. And I am #Christian. #LivingInTruth @maryjosharp

I believe atheists can be moral and do good. I differ from atheists when it comes to establishing a source of goodness. #LivingInTruth @maryjosharp

I don't believe science is the only way to know truth. There are things science cannot tell us: ethics, logic. #LivingInTruth

No method of #science can prove that the methods of science are the only way to know #truth. #LivingInTruth

A worldly mindset seeks to only #bless those who bless them. #Jesus commands us to be better in #tolerance than this worldly view. #LivingInTruth

What is #truetolerance? #LivingInTruth @maryjosharp

Jesus laid the ground rules for #truetolerance. Luke 6:27-36 #LivingInTruth

Do #good and evil exist? #LivingInTruth

How do you know #good and evil exist? #LivingInTruth

What is your standard of #goodness? #LivingInTruth

Just like a builder uses his plumb line to establish a true vertical, humans need a plumb line to establish true goodness. #LivingInTruth

DAY ONE

CONVERSATION GOAL: To use questions to respond to a situation or statement that models the Lord and is helpful for productive conversation

I used to teach band in the public school system. One day, when I was still a young teacher, I showed up to rehearse my middle school bands on the stage at the high school auditorium. As several busloads of hyper middle school students with musical instruments began to file into the auditorium, the choir director stormed onto the stage, noticeably upset. He angrily informed me that I could not use the stage to rehearse my groups. He needed the stage for his choirs.

I was in quite a pickle. I had used the district calendar to reserve the stage for my bands because we had a concert at that venue later in the evening. However, I could see that stating this fact wasn't going to be fruitful and might just elevate his anger. I was even more concerned because my students were now watching.

I had extremely limited time to rehearse. So I was at a loss for what to do, but I needed to do something fast.

What do you think you would have done in this situation?

Instead of attempting to manage the director's anger and argue my case for district calendaring, I asked him a question. My question was geared at helping him work through the situation.

I had a feeling that if I launched into a defense of how I had scheduled and cleared this rehearsal, it wouldn't do much good. He appeared committed to his assumption about the situation; after all, he did

come into the auditorium already angry (and I didn't really know him). So I asked, "What would you do in my situation?"

Asking him this question helped him to uncover the basic problems in the situation. The biggest problem was insufficient venues for our multiple performing groups in the district. He decided to leave us to use the stage, since the basic problem was not solvable in this moment. I was just the recipient of his frustration. In asking him to help me work through the situation, the fire he initially directed towards me (and my students) was sufficiently deflected.

Many times Jesus used questions to either deflect the fire of those with whom He engaged or as a way of helping the person uncover his own beliefs.

In Matthew 21:23-27 what did the religious leaders ask Jesus?

How did Jesus respond to the leaders?

What was the end result?

The chief priests and elders approached Jesus with an aggressive question about His ministry and identity. They asked him to provide His credentials for His teaching, healing, and judging.

Jesus, however, recognized that these men intended to trap Him. He chose not to give them fuel for their fire. Instead, He asked these men a question in return and promised "an answer for an answer."[1]

Jesus wasn't avoiding their question, but He knew if they answered His question, they would inadvertently answer their own as well—similar to solving the situation with the choir director.

Think back over your last month and choose an occasion when you had a high-tension encounter with someone about something. The example could be trivial or crucial. We just want to learn and practice.

If you were having the encounter again, how might you have used questions to defuse or improve the conversation?

In the encounter with the religious leaders, Jesus used a question to deflect the heat of a fiery attack. Other times, though, He used questions as a way to get the person to think about his own assumptions and beliefs.

In Luke 9:18-20, what is the first question Jesus asked?

What is the second question Jesus asked?

Why do you think Jesus didn't just give a teaching on this matter?

Jesus frequently used questions to teach the crowds as well as to train His own disciples. In this passage, Jesus first asked what the general population thought of Him. The responses showed the general speculation of the crowds. Notice they made no mention of the Messiah.

Then Jesus asked a question to uncover the personal belief of the disciples. "Who do you say that I am?" Peter responds with, "God's Messiah!" or "You are the Christ!"

We, likewise, can use questions to uncover the beliefs of the people with whom we converse. Discovering their beliefs, and helping them clarify those beliefs, opens opportunities for productive dialog.

Though Jesus employed the overt use of questioning to get at the underlying belief of the individual, He also used more subtle questions at times. See the story of the rich young ruler (Mark 10:17-27). Jesus used questions in this conversation in two different situations.

What can you learn from Jesus' example about conversation?

What do you think are some of the reasons Jesus used questions instead of answers?

DEFUSE THE TENSION BOMB: Instead of allowing defensiveness and anger to well up and take over your conversations, you can diffuse tense situations by asking a question.

DAY TWO

CONVERSATION GOAL: To learn to use questions to examine a statement

PEOPLE TEND TO TRADE ONLY
CONCLUSIONS, NOT HOW DIFFERENT
PARTIES ARRIVED AT THEIR CONCLUSIONS.[2]
— TIM MUELHOFF

4

Asking conversational questions—a seemingly simple task—requires a bit more nuance than what we might think. One reason is that most people, in my experience, haven't spent a lot of time thinking through what they believe and why they believe it. So rather than feeling safe to offer responses to questions, some people will go into defensive mode out of a lack of knowledge or confidence. Others may react with disgust or even indignation, feeling that your questions are too personal and private because you are discussing religious beliefs. Take a moment to think back through some of your previous conversations on belief in God.

Think of the last time you asked someone a question about belief in God. What did you ask?

What prompted the question?

What was the result of your question or was there any result of which you can remember?

Questions are one way human beings learn about and communicate with their world. They are not just the tool of the modern religious skeptic; rather, questions are a tool for any learner in nearly any situation. When we enter into a conversation about truth, we enter into a learning situation. However, a crucial element to having a good conversation, is making the environment safe for meaningful discussion. So let's take some time to refresh our questioning ability, since effectively using questions to uncover truth takes practice and patience.

Let's say you invited me over for dinner. I bring with me an unmarked brown paper bag, which I set on the table and have left unopened throughout the course of our evening together. As the night is drawing to a close, your curiosity about the bag has become insatiable. What do you do?

1) Give me the reasons for why you believe there is nothing in the bag.

2) State that you believe X is in the bag and that I should confess X is in there as well.

3) Expound on the evils of unmarked brown bags brought to dinner parties.

4) Tell me that in order to experience the fullness of the contents of the bag, I must first surrender my life to opening the bag.

5) Your response, if not one of the above:

Wouldn't you ask me a question to gain some knowledge about the brown bag mystery? So imagine you ask, "What's in the bag?" and I respond with, "Whatever you think is in the bag is good for you, and whatever I think is in the bag is good for me." Now what would you do?

Although I'm imagining some of my friends would be tempted to smack me upside the head for purposeful ambiguity intended to frustrate them, what would they do if I seemed serious in my response?

Can you think of a problem with saying that the contents of the bag are whatever either of us thinks it to be?

We have a problem. The truth of the brown bag contents cannot just be whatever an individual thinks it is. The brown bag contains something, and you now want to know the truth about the contents. So you are faced with having to make another conversation choice in your brown bag mystery: Do you demand to see the contents? Do you lecture me on my seemingly evasive behavior? Do you ask a further question?

Which of these options would have the most productive effect creating a safe environment to induce further conversation or is there another option? (No physical violence allowed in my learning activity.)

After choosing your option, write out what you would say.

Most likely the first two options are going to shut down the conversation and you won't get to the truth you seek. However, if you were to ask me a question, I would most likely continue to engage in conversation—particularly if you asked thoughtfully, genuinely, and with respect.

While the brown bag mystery seems a frivolous (if not slightly annoying) example, we can apply the same concepts over to discussing not-so-frivolous matters such as discovering a person's beliefs about God.

Let's imagine that you've invited me over for dinner again. This time, instead of bringing a mysterious brown bag, I've brought a mixed bag of beliefs about God. You are pretty sure that I don't believe in God—or at least not in the God of the Bible—and even though we've had some conversation on the matter, I haven't "opened the bag'" tonight. Your desire to know what I believe has become insatiable. You say to me, "I know we've said some things before, but what do you really believe about God?" I respond with, "Whatever you think about God is good for you, and whatever I think about God is good for me. That is what I think."

Note that this idea may also be stated in the following forms and variations:

- Whatever a person believes about God is equally true.
- I try not to judge a person's view of God since I don't think you can know the truth about God.
- All religions teach the same thing and therefore are equally true for the person who believes them.

How would you respond to my statement? Be prepared to share your answers with your group.

I would ask, "What do you mean by that?" This would be the first question I almost always ask in this situation. I may have some assumptions about the person, her mixed bag of beliefs, and her response. However, I actually do not know if my understanding matches her own understanding of that statement unless I ask.

CONFIDENCE BUILDER: The Brown Bag Mystery cannot logically end with the contents are whatever is good for you and whatever is good for me. Neither can it be what an individual may think it to be in accordance with their background (maybe where they grew up brown bags always indicated lunches, or alcohol, or even more insidious things). Knowing me, I probably brought some books over for you in that brown bag or maybe even a snack! And though there is a truth to be found in this mystery, if you begin to lose your cool or become aggressive, I may care more about protecting myself from you than I care about the truth. As the authors of *Crucial Conversations* state, "Dialogue calls for the free flow of meaning—period. And nothing kills the flow of meaning like fear. When you fear that people aren't buying into your ideas, you start pushing too hard. When you fear that you may be harmed in some way, you start withdrawing and hiding. Both these reactions—to fight and to take flight—are motivated by the same emotion: fear. On the other hand, if you make it safe enough, you can talk about almost anything and people will listen. If you don't fear that you're being attacked or humili-

ated, you yourself can hear almost anything and not become defensive."[3] Remember that the problem in conversation is not typically the content, but the condition of the conversation.

You could use many questions in this situation. Let's look at some others:

What are your reasons for thinking that?

Why do you believe that is true?

Why do you find that to be the case?

How do you know that?

How did you come to that understanding about God?

How have you come to this conclusion?

From where are you getting that?

How would you describe the difference between asking the questions above in a way that would further conversation and asking these questions in a way that would hinder the conversation?

What are some specific things you can do to avoid hindering the conversation when asking these questions?

Asking a good question in the right way will allow both you and the other person to better understand her statement. Some practical steps you can take towards asking "the right way" are:

1) Take a personal inventory on your motives for engaging in conversation: What are your goals and what do you hope to gain? (Week Three)

2) Pay attention to the attitude you are broadcasting in tone of voice and body language: Are you monitoring yourself and the other person for safety-in-conversation violations (fear, aggression, defensiveness, condescension)?

3) Trust Jesus with this person and/or this conversation (in prayer and in the moment).

4) Be grateful to God that He has entrusted you with someone He greatly loves

Further, we are not just going to look for the "what do you believe," but also the "why do you believe that."

As we learned in Week Three, the statements we hear from people are never formed in a vacuum of objective, unbiased inquiry.

I have read posts and articles by some atheists who seem to think such a vacuum is possible as if science, logic, and evidence exist in some separate realm that is untainted by human emotion, desire, and perceptions. As author, Tim Muelhoff, writes, "What a person believes is deeply entwined with his or her personal and social history."[4]

Why do we need to understand the influences that have shaped a person in order to have meaningful and productive conversations with them?

In the story of Jesus and the Samaritan woman at the well, we see that Jesus didn't just ask about her beliefs; He also included her story. A person's background is very much a part of their current view of the world. Therefore, to discover the fuller understanding of their belief, we need to get more of the story than just a one-line zinger or sound bite. We need to understand the shaping influences of a person's life to better understand a person's argument.

Have they just picked up assumptions without examining them? Are their opinions really their own? How committed to the ideas are they? What challenges to their ideas have they already faced? What is the emotional intent they bring to the conversation? While we don't ask these questions directly, these are the kinds of questions we're seeking to answer.

For the next three days, we'll walk through three prominently held ideas about the truth about God and we'll practice using the approach of questioning to discover a person's beliefs and why she believes it.

CONFIDENCE BUILDER: Typically in a conversation, we are going to use open questions, rather than closed. Closed questions are those that call for short, bare minimum answers like "yes" or "no." Closed questions are used to check a person's understanding, find out a specific fact, or conclude a discussion: "How old are you?" "Do you eat strawberries?" "Did you understand what I told you?" An open question prompts a longer reply as it inquires into a person's opinions, feelings, and knowledge while leaving the structure of the response up to the individual. It opens up the conversation and that's our target. We want to discover what a person believes is true and create an environment in which it is safe for that person to tell us. I shoot for this goal even when the other person obviously does not share my concern for respect and openness.

CONVERSATION GOAL: To effectively question the statement, "Science is the only way to know truth."

I was flying home from a conference in New Jersey feeling rather worn out. I had fallen asleep for around 15 minutes and when I awoke, the man next to me—a nervous flyer—began to talk to me about my work. When he realized that I make arguments for the existence of God, he told me there was no empirical evidence for God. That's a pretty bold statement. Rebuttals to and thoughts about his statement began swirling around in my head.

What would be your response? Put yourself in my shoes for a moment. We're on a plane with people all around. I don't know the man, and I don't want to come across as rude or ignorant.

I imagine this man had been able to stump a few Christians by utilizing the term *empirical evidence* in conversations about God. Perhaps even just now you thought, *empirical—what does that mean?* Conversely, you may have some experience in answering such claims, and you may have thought up numerous responses to his statement.

It may not surprise you by now to learn that I responded with, "What do you mean by that?"

What benefit might come from asking a question instead of jumping right into a refutation of this man's statement? (Look back over the first two days this week, if needed.)

By asking the man what he meant, I received this response, "We can only know what our senses tell us." Again, my thoughts raced towards refuting his statement, but I wanted to discover at least one more thing about his view before I responded. So I asked him, "How do you know that?"

He looked as though he was searching for an answer but came up short. So after waiting a bit, I clarified my question, "What is your grounding for thinking your senses give you truth about reality?"

Consider my question for a moment: How do you know your senses accurately report what they see, hear, smell, touch, and taste to your mind? Can you think of an answer for the man?

Write your response here or perhaps write that you have no response.

Would you be able to use any of your senses (taste, touch, smell, hear, feel) to verify that the senses are the only way to know things? If so, which one(s) and why? If not, why not?

Can we verify by any scientific means that the senses are the only way to know things? Why?

The man got angry, cursed, and said, "I don't know." My question uncovered that he had made an assertion for which he had no substantial basis. Further, the assumption that the senses are the only way to know things is a philosophical assumption, it is not empirically verifiable. For more, see the article on "Science and Faith: Two Arguments."

Through years of talking with people about their beliefs, I have found that many people have ideas and beliefs for which they've never attempted to find significant or substantial support. It's not just folks who do not believe in God, either. I've run into a number of Christians who cannot give reasoning for why they believe in God or for why they believe a certain thing about God. I must include myself in this number at times.

Further, notice that the man got angry enough to curse at me. Weren't we just talking about impassionate scientific evidence as gained through the human senses? What triggered anger? I hadn't been rude or aggressive, so, at first, I had no idea why he got angry and I was actually taken off guard. Rather than becoming defensive or shying away from his anger, I gave him a breather, sat quietly, and made sure my body language wasn't unapproachable.

The man then apologized for his profanity. Eventually, he disclosed that the church had emotionally hurt him in his childhood. I discerned that he used anger from that early experience to fuel his pursuit of intellectual dissent for most of his life. (He looked to be around 50.) Within three questions, I had disrupted his life-long pattern of thought.

Do you remember the Tim Muelhoff quote from yesterday? What did he say about what a person believes?

How does this quote help you understand the gentleman's sudden anger towards me? Or does it?

We humans are never operating in a vacuum. We cannot achieve a state in which we develop a view that is completely void of emotional influences, social influences, family backgrounds, and biases. We all have a complex environmental mixture of these things. These influences shape our current thoughts and beliefs.

So when someone uses the "science is the only way to know truth" objection to belief in God, be aware that this objection is still subject to all the same social influences as any other belief. Merely, tossing in the word "science," or a scientific term, doesn't make a person's belief more or less true than yours.

CONFIDENCE BUILDER: "Empirical evidence"
The Merriam-Webster Online Dictionary defines empirical evidence as "1: originating in or based on observation or experience <*empirical* data> 2: relying on experience or observation alone often without due regard for system and theory <an *empirical* basis for the theory> 3: capable of being verified or disproved by observation or experiment <*empirical* laws>."[5]

We can take it to mean that empirical evidence is that which we can observe. Note that the term doesn't particularly refer to evidence from a one-time, non-repeatable event, since that kind of event cannot be observed over and over. However, Jesus walked the earth for forty days after rising from the dead. Those who were with Him had an opportunity to empirically verify His resurrection on multiple occasions during that time (as some did).[6]

My questioning helped the man on the plane to get to the source of his belief. In this case, the source wasn't really his belief in science as the sole bearer of truth. Rather, he had a belief formed on the foundation of hurtful experiences in the church. The questions drew the line back to the hurt, rather than the science. I needed to be willing and able to minister to a hurting person, even though that person came across as a well-put-together and strong-minded individual.

What would you do next in the conversation? The man has said he didn't know the response, cursed at you, and now gave an apology. What's your move?

4

At this point, I asked if I could share my reasoning for thinking the senses give us accurate information about the universe in which we live. I told him that if there is a Creator God, and this God is the personal and relational God of the Bible, then it would be reasonable to say that He created in us faculties by which we can know more about Him. For example, Genesis tells us we're made in the image of God (Gen. 1:27), who is the giver of truth (John 14:6; 16:13; 18:37). Part of that image is the ability to know truth. It is rational to say that if there is a God, then He made us with the ability to know and understand truth for the purpose of knowing and understanding something about God. Finding truth is not an easy endeavor, but we are capable—even with all our social influences. So the scientific endeavor makes sense firmly grounded within the Christian view of God and man.

VERBAL GIFT CARD: "The scientific endeavor makes sense when firmly grounded within the Christian view of God and man. I am a resolute/positive supporter of gaining knowledge and truth about our universe through the methods of science."

Take a few minutes to check where you are emotionally. Are you excited, frustrated, indifferent, or other? For some of us, today's material is a bit hard to follow. Are you currently telling yourself that this material is too difficult or that you aren't smart enough to talk with people about hard subjects?

If so, what do you think is the source of those thoughts?

During conversation, or even before engaging, we tend to do some internal talk. We may tell ourselves things that hinder conversation with others, such as "I'm not smart enough to discuss this subject," or "I don't want to look like a fool." I'm addressing these thoughts because I have heard them from women all over the country at my events. If you currently feel that engaging in the science and faith conversation would be about as burdensome as digging up a woolly mammoth, then I encourage you to pray about the source of your feelings. If our enemy can silence the people of truth, he can enslave the multitudes. Though we all have different learning styles and abilities, we can all have conversation with people from our current level of knowledge. So let's discover some practical steps we can take when someone uses a statement like "science is the only way to know truth" or "we no longer need to believe in God because science has disproved God"?

1) Name some assumptions that could be the source of this statement. This step is for building your confidence in asking the first question.

2) Be ready to ask a question. Write one below.

3) What response might you get to your question?

4) What's your next move? (Ask another question, give a quick response)

As we wrap up today, call to mind an increasingly popular definition of science: it is a tool we use to understand the natural and physical universe. If that is the definition, then science cannot investigate that which is not physical ... such as ethics, logic, and philosophy. (And we would possibly lose the fields of science that are not based in strictly physical matter, such as psychology.) So we could not even prove that science is a good thing or that science is an endeavor that gives us truth without approaching the scientific endeavor from a philosophical viewpoint.

FOR FURTHER STUDY

For further reading on this matter, see Christian philosopher, J.P. Moreland's works:

Scaling the Secular City: A Defense of Christianity, Chapter 7 "Science and Christianity"

Christianity and the Nature of Science

You may also visit these webpages on science and faith:

The Veritas Forum
questions.veritas.org/science-faith

Oxford Professor, John Lennox's website
johnlennox.org/resources

Bethinking.org
www.bethinking.org/does-science-disprove-god

DAY FOUR

CONVERSATION GOAL: To effectively question the belief that we can find good apart from God

Back in January of 2009, the British Humanist Society, with the sponsorship of atheist Oxford University professor Richard Dawkins, began to run ads on buses in London claiming, "There's probably no God. Now stop worrying and enjoy your life." The campaign was an attempt to brighten up the image of traditional atheism, which has typically had a more gloomy outlook on life.

Do you think atheism may have an image problem? Explain why or why not:

As atheist editorialist, Julian Baginni, describes, "The atheist stereotype has been one of the dark, brooding existentialist gripped by the angst of a purposeless universe." He states that this is understandable, since "atheists have to live with the knowledge that there is no salvation, no redemption, no second chances. Lives can go terribly wrong in ways that can never be put right."[7]

However, while atheism is a commitment to this bleak outlook, the British Humanist Association, along with maybe an atheist you know, continues to portray its beliefs as liberating and even goes so far as to suggest that atheism is ultimately good for mankind.

You might hear someone reflecting the results of this image campaign with a statement like, "I don't need God to be good." Today, let's learn to question this idea, so that you can uncover the source of such a belief.

What could you ask an atheist who claimed that atheism was a bright outlook on life?

What could you ask an atheist who claimed "to be good, we don't need God"?

As I stated in yesterday's session, I usually start off with the question, "What do you mean by that?" You can vary this question by asking: "Can you explain to me what you mean by saying that to be good, we don't need God?" "Can you explain why you think atheism offers a bright outlook on life?" Plus, you can always modify questions to reflect that which sounds more authentically like you. Remember, our goal is to get clarification for ourselves as well as for the person with whom we are speaking.

I'll get a variety of responses to both questions, but typically the responses center on the idea that people don't have to believe in God to be good or live morally. I agree with the person on this point because they are right: anyone can do good things or behave morally (Rom. 2:14-16). What I want to know is how a person is determining what is good and what is not good.

What question could you ask a person about how they know what is good and what is not good?

I would most likely ask a person a "how do you know that" type question. I might say, "How do you know that something is good or not good?" Here are three of the responses I have received:

1) The culture in which you live determines what is good for your people.
2) The more humans progress in knowledge the more we understand what is good for all people.
3) Every individual must decide for herself what is good.

Write a follow-up question, or two, for each one of these responses.

I'll most likely follow up with: Why do you believe that? Or, from where are you getting that?

One of the most important discussions when it comes to good and evil is finding the source or standard of goodness. The reason it is so important to find the source is because most people live as though good and evil—right and wrong—have some kind of real existence that good and evil are not just delusions of our minds. Our daily choices, thoughts, and actions are wrapped up in determining whether or not something is actually good for us. Yet, where are we getting this idea that anything is "good" at all? Within an atheist view, there is no standard to determine what is good and what is not good.

Let's briefly look at the responses above and some problems associated with them:

#1. Though a culture may decide what works for their own people, that decision may not be what is good for all people (remember subjectivity). Today, we'll discover this problem when considering the actions and beliefs of the Nazi Regime.

#2. Human knowledge does not necessarily result in an increase in goodness or in moral progress.

Rather, some things we learn seem to pose a challenge for our goodness, such as what to do with the knowledge of how to split atoms or how to freeze fertilized human embryos. Humans can also gain false knowledge, which complicates finding goodness and truth.

#3. If every person individually decides what is good, then no individual's way of doing things could be ultimately wrong, even if it led to the taking of human life (think sociopath, psychopath, murder, rapist, narcissist, and so on). What's good for one person may be drastically bad for another ... but who's to judge if everyone decides what is good?

For example, one human may think creating a race of genetically superior human beings is good. He may then proceed to rid the earth of genetically inferior humans. Another human may believe that it is good to see all people as equally valuable and fight adamantly against ridding the earth of inferior humans. These views of "good" would have drastically different results for mankind. The first view was not hypothetical but an actual description of the people in favor of Nazi Germany's eugenics and racial cleansing programs.

If every individual decides what is good, then how would a person determine which view above is actually good for all mankind?

If no final standard exists to which all people are accountable, then good and evil become subjective to each individual, country, culture, or belief system. There would be no way to give a verdict on goodness that is true for all people. However, most of the people with whom I have spoken who are not believers in God tell me that mankind, void of God, is capable of determining and establishing goodness for everyone.

King Solomon in Ecclesiastes reflected on this problem of establishing good and evil for all mankind, when he considered what the world would be like if there was no God; he considered "everything under the sun."

How would you describe what Solomon saw when he looked upon the world (Eccl. 3:16-22)?

What did Solomon observe next (Eccl. 4:1-3)?

What did he say about the oppressed?

According to Ecclesiastes 4:2-3, what did Solomon conclude about life in light of the amount and extent of great evil "under the sun"?

In these passages, Solomon, the wise king, considers this worldly life apart from God and sees great injustice and oppression. He sees those who are powerful abusing the oppressed and he laments that no one cares for or comforts those being abused. He concludes that if this life is all that there is then it is better to never have lived at all.

"So I admired the dead, who have already died, more than the living, who are still alive. But better than either of them is the one who has not yet existed, who has not seen the evil activity that is done under the sun" (Eccl. 4:2-3). He cries out, that all life is "vanity of vanities;" all is meaningless! We live and we die like the animals, both returning to the dust from which we came (Eccl. 3:19-20).

This bleak outlook of Solomon is how he viewed good and evil in a world void of God. It is an honest look at the situation of mankind if no God exists to be the standard of goodness for all.

How did the apostle reflect something of the same idea in 1 Corinthians 15:14-19?

Notice, that Solomon's reflection in Ecclesiastes conveys an atheistic world view, and Paul's statement reflects the tragic consequences if Jesus did not rise from the grave. Contrary to the "stop worrying and enjoy your life" attitude of the atheist image campaign, Solomon and Paul's reflections more aptly acknowledge the total situation of mankind across the world. Great injustice and oppression characterize this world. The situation demands greater investigation than a simple, positive slogan can provide.

As Baginni points out, atheists can live meaningful, moral, and happy lives, but he emphasizes that though they can live that way, they have no way of knowing if their lives are meaningful, moral, and happy or if they even should be so.

How would you explain the difference between living a moral life and determining of what a moral life consists?

What is the difference between living a moral life and determining why a life should be lived with morals?

Why are these differences so important in our conversation about truth, goodness, and God?

How does God's goodness impact our understanding and practice of morality?

In conversation about human goodness, we need a standard, or plumb line, of goodness that all people can utilize in checking their individual views to see what is actually good. Just like a builder uses his plumb line to establish a true vertical, humans need a plumb line to establish true goodness. Without a plumb-line or a standard we really have nothing to discuss, for each person could decide for themselves what is good and evil. With no standard outside of each person's view no way remains to prescribe what humans should do. While someone might say, "Well, that's just kooky. Doctors tell us all the time what we should do … for example, what we should do to live a healthy life." Sure, but the doctor is assuming that life should be lived, right? From where did she get that idea?

Christians would say that since God, the author and source of goodness, created life and called His creation "good," we have a source for why we believe we should live rather than die. What is the source for the idea that life is good if you adhere to an atheist world view?

In atheism, the endeavor to find a standard of goodness is futile. No unchanging plumb line guides a person to say, "This is how I know something is good," or "I should do this because it is good." As a result, in atheism, the most vocal or powerful people may end up as the determining voice for what is good for everyone else. Yet, many people I encounter do not even stop to think from where their idea of goodness comes. Is it from the state, the law, the culture, their parents, or their friends? Is it from an actual study on what is good?

In Ecclesiastes, Solomon saw the power some used over others as oppression. He also saw the great injustices that come as a result. Solomon determined that it was better not to exist in this kind of world.

In Christianity, the plumb line is the nature of God. His perfect goodness forms the basis by which we can know anything is good or not good. So when a person says, "I don't need God in order to be good," we need to ask some questions.

PRACTICE EXERCISES:

1) **First, name any assumptions of which you can think that could be the source of the statement "I don't need God to be good." This step is for building your confidence in asking a question.**

2) **Be ready to ask a question. Write at least two clarifying questions you might ask. Try to think of different questions from the ones you wrote earlier.**

3) What response might you get to your question?

4) What's your next move? (Ask another question, give a quick response)

I have been asked many times how I get into serious discussions about belief in God. I can honestly say that questioning how a person determines what is good is one of the most frequent ways I get into conversations about God. Here are some examples:

1: We need a change in the economic direction of our country.

2: What do you mean by that?

1: I mean the system we have now is corrupt, rewarding those who do evil.

2: How do you know that?

1: Just look around you: the rich are getting richer and the poor are getting poorer.

2: How do you know that this system is evil versus good?

1: I don't understand. Are you just messing with me? It's obvious.

2: No. I actually think you believe something good exists to be put into practice for our economic situation, but I want to know how you determine what is good.

1: Everyone knows what is good.

2: I'm so sick of our stupid teachers at school treating me so unfairly.

1: What do you mean?

2: I'm always getting in trouble when I've done nothing wrong. It's so unfair.

1: How are you getting treating unfairly?

2: Well, take my history class: Bonnie sits in the back and when she talks, the teacher never says anything. I sit near the middle and when I talk, I always get called out in front of the class.

1: What makes this treatment unfair?

2: All students should be treated equally! I can't even believe you asked that!

1: I don't understand where you get the idea that all students should be treated equally. Where are you getting that idea from?

Both conversations are now primed to move into how a person knows what is good and what is evil. Everyday conversations actually provide many opportunities to discuss our beliefs about God.

For further practice, you can use the above conversations and continue the dialog with a partner or write out what you think would happen next. How would you communicate a belief in God as the standard of goodness in either of these situations?

You may also wish to use a recent conversation or controversy in which you were involved and write out how you could effectively question a person's standard of goodness.

CONVERSATION GOAL: To question the remark that Christians are intolerant

Imagine you've applied for a job with a Norwegian company and you finally received a response. As you begin to read the letter, you notice that the company has rejected your application. However, instead of simply ending with a "Thank you" or "Sincerely, Com-

pany X," you notice the company representative has further explained why you did not get the job: that your education is from an "intolerant" Christian university from where they will not employ graduates, citing Christianity as the reason for the destruction of the Norse culture, tradition, and way of life. Once the initial shock of the aggressive response has begun to die down, you begin to think on how you should address this matter.

How do you handle the situation? Here's some options:

- You write the company a letter explaining their deficient knowledge of the Nordic and Christian histories.
- You immediately contact a lawyer intending to sue the company.
- You yell and scream at home, devising retributive schemes you don't intend to pursue.
- You go out for chocolate cake and ice cream. (A little comfort food, right?)

What would you do?

This scenario may seem ridiculous, but it is one that actually happened to a graduate of Trinity Western University in Canada. The young woman whose application was turned down by a Norwegian hiking company, found herself in a series of ugly email exchanges with representatives of the company. Her initial response leaned towards the first option above.

One problem with jumping into an answer rather than asking a question is that if the audience is already on guard and defensive, they are probably not going to listen to anything you have to say. In this case, the young woman's response only further incited the company leaders and their emails to her became even more offensive. Instead of jumping into a refutation, which may or may not go well, a question "brings to the surface the questioner's assumptions."[8]

What question could you ask the hiking company representative to help bring his assumptions to the foreground?

What do you think some of the assumptions of the company representative may be?

Many questions could be used in this situation. With the information given concerning the hiking company's response, I might ask some of these questions:

1) What do you mean by intolerant?

2) Do you mean to say that you would not hire me based on the fact that I am a Christian (even if I met all the qualifications)?

3) Do you mean to say that I am, in some way, responsible for what happened between the Nordic and Christian religions several hundred years ago?

4) What would you do if you received a response letter of this nature to a job application?

5) What would you do if someone turned down your job application with the addendum that they would never hire a Norsemen?

These questions would help the representative and the job applicant understand the basic beliefs inform-

ing his response. For this particular situation, the questions would also aid in protecting the legal rights of the job applicant. She would be interrogating his statements rather than making any claims that might be used against her in a court of law.

SIDE NOTE: This same university decided to create a law program. In response to the request for the program's creation and accreditation, a group of Canadian law associations put together a statement that they would not recognize the degree granted to law graduates of the university due to the university's policy on same-sex marriage.[9] Here we have an instance of intolerance and it is coming from those who are supposed to defend the rights of individuals. See the Confidence Builder on "The Boy Who Cried Wolf."

What other instances of intolerance towards Christians do you see in our culture today? Be prepared to discuss your answer with your group.

Pick some instances of intolerance in our culture. List some questions you could ask if you heard any of these personally.

In your group this week grab a partner and use the instances along with your questions to practice addressing a situation of intolerance.

We need to remember an important goal for this hot topic of intolerance. We, as Christians, need to handle situations in accordance with the teachings of Jesus.

In my daily walk, I encounter Christians who hold to a victim mentality or even an "us" versus "them" attitude when handling intolerance. However, our Scripture tells us quite the opposite.

What does Jesus tell you to do for others according to Matthew 7:12?

What are we to avoid when someone treats us wrongly (evil) according to 1 Peter 3:8-11?

What does this passage say about your words in response to evil?

Not only are we supposed to treat others as we ourselves want to be treated, but we are never to repay evil with evil. We are to be those who bless and seek peace. These are high standards of true tolerance reiterated throughout the New Testament in teachings such as the Sermon on the Mount (Luke 6:27-36).

People of a worldly mindset seek to bless those who bless them. They do good to those who do good to them. Jesus' teaching commands us to be better in tolerance than just this worldly view. We are to seek what is good for those who do not seek what is good for us.

Why do you think we are commanded to do good to others even when those people do not do good to us?

One of the tasks God gave us is to "speak the truth in love" (Eph. 4:15, NLT). He has not been caught off guard by the gross levels of human sin and how we treat one another (remember Ecclesiastes?).

God knows that when we are reviled and respond in love we are trusting in Him rather than in the ways of the world. He knows how difficult such responses are for us. Remember that Jesus "in every respect has been tempted as we are, yet without sin" (Heb. 4:15, ESV). Think of how God tolerates us in all our sin because He values us infinitely.

Tolerance is all about people. We tolerate people. This is a vital distinction we must make when speaking of tolerance in our society. Real tolerance is not about the equality of all beliefs or religions or ideologies. Tolerance is about the equality of people despite our disagreements with various beliefs and religions and ideologies.

Because this concept is so important, take time to carefully paraphrase the previous paragraph. Think how you would explain this understanding of tolerance.

True tolerance is putting up with the person who holds an idea or belief, etc., with whom you do not agree. If we lose this view of tolerance, we will begin to marginalize people due to their various views. A great way to help people see that they are perhaps marginalizing others is to ask them, "Do you consider yourself a tolerant person?" And follow that up with, "What is your definition of tolerance?"

Write a definition of *tolerance* you can use in conversation:

4

How can asking a question about a person's view be an act of true tolerance?

What would you hope to see happen in the case of the girl who applied to the Norwegian hiking company?

How can you pray for those whose eyes have been closed to true tolerance?

FOR FURTHER STUDY
Paul Copan. *True For You, But Not for Me: Deflating the Slogans that Leave Christians Speechless.* Chapters 5 & 6

Francis Beckwith & Greg Koukl. *Relativism: Feet Firmly Planted in Mid-Air*

You may also view these webpages on tolerance:

Stand to Reason Ministries, "Tolerance," *http://www.str.org/*

BeThinking.org, "Pluralism, Relativism, and Tolerance," *http://www.bethinking.org*

CONFIDENCE BUILDER: "The Boy Who Cried Wolf" In one of the most famous of Aesop's fables, a shepherd boy had the job to tend the village's flock of sheep. However, the boy grows bored and decides to stir up the village by crying out that a wolf was attacking the sheep. He did this several times before the villagers decide not to trust him any more. One day, a wolf does attack the sheep and the shepherd cries out for help, but no one trusts his warning.

Our culture is in danger of crying wolf with intolerance. When so many people loosely throw the term around to describe any situation involving something of which they disagree, the term begins to lose its meaning and, therefore, its power to rightfully address ethical problems. Unlike the shepherd's flagrant use of wolf, I don't believe most people employ the term with deceitful intent. However, much like the damage done to the shepherd's sheep, in the end, we will find this wolf-crying to have done great harm to our own communities when real attacks of intolerance should be stopped.

INTOLERANCE & HATE SPEECH

"FOR THE POWER OF MAN TO MAKE HIMSELF WHAT HE PLEASES MEANS, AS WE HAVE SEEN, THE POWER OF SOME MEN TO MAKE OTHER MEN WHAT THEY PLEASE."[10] – C.S. LEWIS

C.S. Lewis cautioned that as a society lets go of an objective basis for morality, it ends up conditioned to believe the values and preferences of a few men. He called these "the conditioners." They are those with power, a voice, and the platform to spread their message. While his warning sounds like the introduction of a fictitious dystopian novel, it appears that our society has reached the dawn of dystopia.

Lewis' social conditioners are those who prescribe for everyone the values they have chosen for themselves. Rather than ethics chosen according to any objective basis or standard, these values are subjectively chosen. Yet, anyone who disagrees with the conditioners could be labeled as bigoted, ignorant, and perhaps, dangerous. In our society, we are seeing what it means when the few decide what the rest of us may or may not discuss or even think. This new conditioning emanates, in part, from a redefining of the term *hate speech*.

The US Legal website defines *hate speech* as "a communication that carries no meaning other than the expression of hatred for some group, especially in circumstances in which the communication is likely to provoke violence. It is an incitement to hatred primarily against a group of persons defined in terms of race, ethnicity, national origin, gender, religion, sexual orientation, and the like. Hate speech can be any form of expression regarded as offensive to racial, ethnic and religious groups and other discrete minorities or to women."[11]

Notice that hate speech is communication that carries no meaning other than the expression of hatred. One website described these words as *fighting words*, or words meant to intentionally incite violence. Fighting words have a different motive than public debate on a hot or controversial topic.

With so many different views in our society, we must walk the hate speech line carefully or we could propel ourselves towards a no longer truly free society—one that no longer values freedom itself. The social redefining of hate speech language knowingly or unknowingly affects at least one foundational doctrine of the United States, the freedom of religion. The first amendment prohibition against government establishment of religion was not intended to persecute people of religious beliefs for their views on issues like abortion, homosexuality, or marriage; it was, in so far as possible within the social contract, a safeguard against discrimination, bigotry, and persecution.

After Frank Turek and Michael Shermer held a debate at Stony Brook University on whether God or science better explains morality, a writer charged Turek with hate speech. In his article, the writer claimed Turek should not be allowed a public platform because he did not positively affirm same-sex marriage. Turek's debate contained no fighting words, no communication without meaning, and no communication with the purpose of expressing hatred toward another group. Yet, because Turek does not support same-sex marriage, his critic redefines hate speech to include civil disagreement on a controversial topic. According to the new definition, holding an out of favor opinion, or even refusing to positively affirm the approved opinion, becomes a crime worthy of punishment.

This article is an example of social and verbal bullying. It demonstrates a concerted lack of tolerance. A tolerant and appropriate response to Turek would have included: a lack of negatively charged wording including slander and accusation, a positive case made for the critic's position, a thoughtful analysis of and engagement with Turek's ideas, and a utilization of evidence and logical argumentation. Yet, there's the rub with the redefining of hate speech: the ill-regard of basic logic. When a person can no longer offer logical arguments to oppose another person's view, we find ourselves in a despotic society.

I'm calling for a new rebellion against the shutting down of debate on controversial topics in our society. The new rebellion is for those who will stand up for logic, reason, and the search for truth. The current redefining of hate speech threatens the use of logic and reason in the public realm. It endangers our pursuit of the good, true, and beautiful. We presently need everyday people to stand up for the search for truth.

As responsible citizens in a free society, we must civilly rebel against any change of the definition of hate speech that includes meaningful discussion of potentially offensive topics. We must carefully recognize and teach the difference between debating controversial topics and slinging empty fighting words. Otherwise the vocal few in our society—Lewis' social conditioners—will continue to define as hate speech anything that differs from their own set of values.

Legally, the dissenter's voice has not yet been shut down. Socially, the bullying has begun. Allowing anyone to define what should or should not be discussed publicly to fit their own values and preferences is the height of intolerance. It also reflects a double standard by those who do so in the name of tolerance. Essentially the message is, "We are the tolerant ones, yet we will only tolerate that with which we agree." This message is no tolerance at all. Redefining hate speech cuts the heart out of democracy. Will you be a part of a new rebellion in which you thoughtfully engage in arguments on controversial issues in the face of bullies who would shut down critical thinking and argumentation? Will you stand for true tolerance that protects the free exchange of ideas, even for the person with whom you disagree? Will you do so with gentleness and respect, even when you are misrepresented and verbally attacked? If so, tweet or post something today about how you value the ability in our land to dissent with public opinion and/or to openly and thoughtfully discuss controversial issues. #newrebellion #truetolerance

HERE'S A START ON TWEETS OR POSTS. FOR MORE GO TO:
www.confidentchristianity.blogspot.com.

I stand for true tolerance: the ability to civilly dissent on controversial topics. #newrebellion

I value the freedom to disagree with others on controversial topics. #newrebellion

I value the use of logical arguments in discussing controversies. #newrebellion

I do not believe in shutting down civil public dissension and discussion on difficult moral subjects. #newrebellion

Disallowing a public platform for dissenting views on morally controversial issues is not tolerant. #truetolerance

Shutting down or shouting down public dialog on controversial issues is not tolerant. #truetolerance

Using logical argumentation is vital to discussing sensitive and emotionally charged topics. #newrebellion

Shutting down or shouting down dissenting voices on controversial issues is not moral progress. #truetolerance

RESPOND TO CULTURAL VIEWS

GROUP

KEY CONCEPTS THIS WEEK:
1) gain knowledge for responding well in conversations
2) understand some common false beliefs or misconceptions about Christianity and Christians
3) practice responses to common false beliefs

QUESTIONS FOR DISCUSSION:
1) What is negatively charged wording, and why do we need to steer clear of it as much as possible?

2) How can inflection and timbre affect the way people receive our responses?

3) How is calling Christians unintelligent an attempt to marginalize them and evidence of a character flaw by the name caller? What might you ask people using these tactics against you?

4) What short response could you give a person who says the Bible comes from a pre-scientific culture in which people were prone to believe in the supernatural?

5) What assumptions can you find in the following statements: "Smart people rely solely on scientific evidence for their beliefs. That is why religious people are unintelligent. They would rather have blind faith for which they have no scientific evidence." Why might a person believe these things to be true? Discuss how thinking through the assumptions helps you to focus on the argument rather becoming argumentative.

6) What is a myth? Why do you think people say that Christianity is a man-made myth? From 1 Timothy 1:4; 4:7; and 2 Timothy 4:4, what could you say to the claim that the Bible is myth?

7) What could you ask someone who says the story of Jesus is a copy of the stories of other gods?

8) How can Christians actively and effectively participate in the political realm without sacrificing their public witness to the truth of God?

Free video session downloads available at *www.lifeway.com/LivingInTruth*

CALL TO ACTION:

Since this is our response week, consider responses you might like to share online in regarding the three misconceptions we've studied. Atheist, skeptics, agnostics, and other Christians are most likely struggling with one or more of these views. You can be a voice of redemption and encouragement. Post any of the following statements to any of your social media sites. Also, don't feel constrained to just post my suggestions. You are creative. I'd love to retweet/share some of your original ideas. Remember to tag me. @maryjosharp #LivingInTruth

Misconceptions about the Christian faith can gum-up the process of clearly thinking through Christianity. #LivingInTruth @maryjosharp

Life and death are in the power of the tongue, and those who love it will eat its fruit. Proverbs 18:21 #LivingInTruth @maryjosharp

Our words can destroy or build up lives. @maryjosharp #LivingInTruth

People in the #Bible were not ready to jump to supernatural explanations. #Zechariah refused to believe based on his own understanding of natural laws. #LivingInTruth

People in the #Bible were not ready to jump to #supernatural explanations. #Thomas wasn't willing to believe #Jesus had risen from the dead. #LivingInTruth

Peter proclaims he was not following cleverly devised myth but was an eyewitness to Christ's revelation of His majesty and glory. 2 Peter 1:16-19 #LivingInTruth

It seems too skeptical to distrust something because humans wrote it down. To hold to that skepticism would be to blow up most of our knowledge.#LivingInTruth

One of the most prominent public ways that Christians bring the hypocrisy charge upon ourselves is by our behavior in politics. #LivingInTruth

Christians are not to match our culture's slanderous behavior; to do so is to enslave ourselves to sin. #LivingInTruth

Hypocrisy is a human trait that is not specific to religious believers. Anyone can be a hypocrite. #LivingInTruth

When I was a child, adults used to tell me, "Don't swallow your gum or a gum tree will grow in your stomach." As silly as that sounds now, it was a driving force behind why I wouldn't swallow my gum. The few times I accidently did swallow my gum, I could feel it like a pit in my stomach beginning to plant itself. However, that gum never did produce a gum tree. The adults' warning just wasn't true. Yet, as a child, I never took the time to find out if the adults were telling me the truth.

When people hold to misconceptions or false beliefs about the Christian faith, those beliefs can plant themselves in their mind and gum-up the process of clearly thinking through Christianity. These misconceptions can also create a sticky situation for Christians who want to discuss their beliefs with others. Throughout this week, we will learn how to respond to prominent false beliefs about Christianity and, perhaps, those planted pits of misconception won't grow into a full-fledged trees of false knowledge.

• • • • •

DAY ONE

CONVERSATION GOAL: To recognize that every person can learn to respond well

We face many challenges when responding to others verbally or in written form. The loaded words pervasive in our language form one of the greatest challenges. Loaded words "elicit an emotional response—positive or negative—beyond their literal meaning and can significantly contribute to persuading others to adopt our point of view."[1] However, "persuading others" can mean a myriad of things such as persuading in a strictly negative fashion through inadvertent name-calling or finger pointing.

Read the example below and underline any negative wording you find whether it's a single word or a phrase.

Person A: I'd really like to believe Christianity is true, but I don't want to check my brains at the door.

Person B: Wow. You really don't know anything about the Christian faith.

Person A: I've seen enough to know that only a fool believes there is a Spirit Daddy living in the sky.

Person B: You are just ignorant. Christianity cannot be reduced to such an absurdity. Have you even read the Bible?

Person A: You people are all alike. You put up your blinders as soon as someone challenges what you believe.

Person B: I can't even talk to you. Your heart is too hardened. You're just committed to your lifestyle of selfish desires. You lack a moral compass. It's no wonder you don't see God for who He really is.

The Scriptures contain much about wisdom in relation to our choice of words. What two powers does Proverbs 18:21 name as belonging to the tongue (our words)?

What does it mean to say "and those who love it will eat its fruit"?

To what does Proverbs 12:6 compare the words of the wicked and the words of the upright?

How would you relate these two passages to each other?

Both passages talk about the power of words to speak life or to speak death to others. The Scripture isn't saying our words have magical power. Think rather about the healing one can experience from talking with a counselor. Our words have great power because they influence both ourselves and others.

The Creator spoke the world into being by the power of His words (Heb. 11:3). Though we do not have the creative power to make universes, our words can destroy or build up lives. Our words are so important that the Lord taught us we will give an account of what we say when we stand before Him in judgment (Matt. 12:36-37).

Another challenge we face in responding to others—one that is not so obvious—comes from not what we say but how we say it. Our timbre of voice and inflection of words powerfully impacts our communication. This challenge is so rampant that logicians have named an error in reasoning *the fallacy of inflection.* You can be misunderstood by just changing the sound of your voice or the way you emphasize your words.

Timbre (pronounced "tamber") is the color or tone we use when speaking. All musical instruments have a musical "color" to their sound. We say that an instrument sounds happy, bright, mellow, sad, brassy, brash, strident, and so forth. Voices have the same thing. We can give our words a different meaning by a bright timbre (usually perceived as happy) or by a mellow timbre—perceived as thoughtful or sad or even sarcastic, depending on the situation.

Try saying the sentence below out loud with a bright voice:

DID YOU PICK UP THE GROCERIES?

Say it again out loud with a brash or harsh voice.

What difference would a hearer perceive from the two ways you expressed the same sentence?

The bright timbre reflects the expectation that you believe they have already done what you asked. The brash timbre conveys a sarcasm that you really don't believe they did what you asked. A vast chasm separates the meaning of these two timbres of voice.

Let's use the same sentence and choose to emphasize one word.

Using a mellow, even-toned voice say the sentence out loud, and put emphasis on the word *you*: Did *you* pick up the groceries?

What does emphasizing the *you* imply in this question?

You might convey the idea that you are suspicious whether or not the person was the actual person that got the groceries. It is akin to saying, "Did you pick the groceries up yourself or did you have someone else do it?" By accenting the word *you* in the question you can imply an entirely different meaning.

If this wasn't your intended meaning, you've just committed the fallacy of inflection. The recipient of your question could quite possibly become defensive because the inflection has a residual effect of sounding accusatory and mistrusting. You might rapidly find yourself in a heated argument over the groceries.

With the following sentences, try saying them out loud and changing your timbre. Also accent or emphasize different words to convey different meanings.

• **Do you know where my keys are?**

• **Thank you for that gift.**

• **Well, you look pretty.**

• **What do you believe about God?**

• **So, you don't believe in God.**

What is a person to do when responding to misconceptions about Christianity? Are we supposed to sound like a robot, with even-toned voices that have no trace of inflection? No. That would be awkward and maybe even construed as inappropriate. We can, however, give our timbre and inflection some purposeful attention for the sake of ministering to others.

Remember, our goal this week is to begin responding to some false beliefs and misconceptions about Christianity. The purpose of responding to these challenges is to help others open up to the truth.

How can your timbre of voice and inflection close people off from considering Christianity?

How can emotionally charged words affect your conversation about God?

How do you think you can improve your skills in these areas to make a difference in your conversations with others?

Let's take a moment to reflect on how we've utilized our tongues—including emotionally charged words, timbre, and inflection—to give life or to destroy it. Use Jesus' words from Matthew 15:10-11: "Listen and understand: It's not what goes into the mouth that defiles a man, but what comes out of the mouth, this defiles a man."

How can you apply Jesus' teaching to your responses to people who adamantly oppose your Christian beliefs?

VERBAL GIFT CARD: "I don't think I can answer you right now without coming across as negative. Please give me a moment because I want to answer you more appropriately."

Jake: Myth!= Religion? Oh, right. The myth is someone else's religion, while your religion is someone else's myth. ;)

MJS: "Oh, right. The myth is someone else's religion, while your religion is someone else's myth. ;)" I know you're just having some fun here, but unfortunately many people seem to take this view. Might I request of you to tell me the difference between the two: religion and mythology? For some reason, these two terms are being used synonymously in the 20th and 21st century.

CONVERSATION GOAL: To learn to aptly respond to the false belief that Christianity is only for the unintelligent

It only takes a quick search online to find someone, somewhere touting the idea that Christianity is for unintelligent nincompoops. I frequently find statements to this effect on my various social media sites. Here's a fairly recent one:

Person1: It is a sad, deluded mind that can believe is this ancient, primitive, cave man "blood magic."

MJS: If you want to impact the world for your own belief system and demonstrate the truthfulness of that belief, it seems you should demonstrate a deep understanding of the other beliefs and not attack a straw man of that belief. Of course, it is easier to tear down a straw man ... especially through the use of lots of negatively-charged wording. But that does not make a good argument.

It's not just atheist antagonists online who spout this false belief, you can also find it prevalent in movies and television series. The CBS television comedy *The Big Bang Theory,* portrays the educated physicists on the show as atheist and the uneducated people, such as the main character's mother, as evangelical Christians. The BBC series, *Doctor Who* regularly takes pot shots at Christianity as being for silly, uninformed people.

Can you remember a movie, television show, or article online you've seen that portrayed Christians as unintelligent? Describe the situation.

How did that experience affect you?

How do you think these shows and articles affect others?

5

Before I studied the reasons for my belief in God, I was negatively impacted by these influences. I often felt intimidated to discuss faith in public, sometimes for fear of being viewed as unintelligent, sometimes for fear of coming across as "shoving my religion on others."

Reflect on your past experiences. Have you ever explicitly or implicitly been told you were not smart or that you lacked critical thinking? How did it affect you?

The accusation that Christians are ignorant can stir up some raw emotion from a former experience—even one unrelated to your belief in God—and may bring to light a hurt with which you've been struggling. I cannot count the number of times I have heard Christians tell me that they are "not smart." If this idea is running around in your head, it may keep you from talking

with people about your belief in God due to a concern that you may be made to look foolish by someone you think could be smarter than you.

While I won't be able to go into detail on all the psychological and scriptural reasons for why and how we develop such beliefs about ourselves, we can look at this specific misconception of Christianity from two perspectives:

#1. Character Flaw: Anyone who purposefully makes you feel unintelligent or "lower in intelligence" than themselves has a character flaw. To do so is selfish and ungracious, lacking a charitable attitude. Scripture is clear that those who lack graciousness and charity are not wise. Isaiah goes so far as to pronounce "woe" to them who act in such ways: "Woe to those who are wise in their own opinion and clever in their own sight" (Isa. 5:21). Proverbs 26:12 states that there is more hope for a fool than for the man who is wise in his own eyes.

#2. Marginalization: Anyone using the claim, "Christianity is for the unintelligent" has chosen an off-the-top-of-the-head, shallow approach to the Christian faith, denoting the same uncharitable attitude towards fellow humans as found in the first perspective. The statement marginalizes those people who are Christians, leaving emotional, psychological, and spiritual damage in its wake.

We will respond to the second perspective on this misconception of Christianity. Since the claim is especially hurtful, it may be hard for us to not respond with similar smugness.

We are seeking to develop the communication skills to graciously minister to people, even in difficult situations. The first thing I want to find out in such circumstances is the driving force behind the person's belief. What makes them think the Christian faith is something like committing intellectual suicide? I usually ask, "Why do you believe that?"

Can you think of any reasons a person might hold to this belief?

We'll look at two possible reasons for this belief that I've encountered.

Reason #1. In the pre-scientific world, people were prone to assign divinity to the natural forces of which they had no understanding. For example, they may have believed the lightning and thunder appeared whenever Zeus or Thor was angry. These people may have believed that Osiris or Dionysius died and rose from the dead every year, explaining the crop cycles and the seasons. Therefore, it's easy to see how these people believed stories such as virgin birth and resurrected gods. This is the kind of stuff the ancients were prone to believe. We now know better due to scientific advancements. (Notice the emotionally charged wording "know better.")

Can you think of a question you would ask a person who responded in this way?

I would begin by asking them how they know that the early Christian believers were prone to believe in "this kind of stuff" such as dying and rising gods and virgin births. In other words, "How do you know that?" I may ask a few more questions to see if they've ever read the Bible and/or the Egyptian, Persian, Greek, Norse, etc. mythology.

I can see how a person might think that all ancient people were prone to believe such things because those beliefs did exist in ancient times. However, it seems to be overreaching to suppose that everyone believed in the gods of mythology. Further, when I read the text of the New Testament I find quite a different story. In one text written by Luke, he tells us the story of Zechariah and his wife Elizabeth who had remained barren into their old age.

When an angel of the Lord visits Zechariah and tells him Elizabeth will bear a son, Zechariah firmly refused to believe based on his own understanding of natural laws. He argued that it was not possible for Elizabeth to be pregnant due to their old age. He was so adamant about his refusal to believe in this supernatural event, the text says that the angel struck him mute (Luke 1:5-25). At the very least, the story shows us that the people in the Bible were not ready to jump to supernatural explanations. Rather, Zechariah resisted even when an angel appeared to him.

Let's go further: Read from Luke's other text, Acts 23:1-8.

For what belief did Paul say that he was being judged?

Why did a dispute break out between the Pharisees and the Sadducees?

In this passage, we have another story about people who would be considered very religious: the two groups of religious authorities in Israel, the Pharisees and the Sadducees. A dispute broke out between the two groups because the Sadducees did not believe in the resurrection. According to verse 8, the Sadducees also did not believe in angels or spirits.

Here we have an example of ancient religious people—in fact, religious ruling authorities responsible for teaching and leading others—who violently defended a position of disbelief in the resurrection and/or other spiritual things. (Luke reports that the dispute became violent.)

Plus, we can find further instances of people who weren't willing to jump to supernatural conclusions until they had substantive evidence.

- Joseph wasn't willing to believe that Mary was supernaturally pregnant.
- Thomas wasn't willing to believe Jesus had risen from the dead.

Both needed evidence; both received significant proof before they accepted supernatural facts. The Bible is not full of jump-to-conclusions kinds of stories. Rather, we find people who know and understand natural ways and are hard-pressed to believe that God is working in the world. They sound very much like people today.

What short response could you give to a person who says the Bible comes from a pre-scientific culture in which people were prone to believe in the supernatural? Plan to discuss your responses with your group this week.

Very important: Practice responses out loud. Try changing timbre and inflection. Be on the lookout for negatively charged wording. Note that others usually detect these charged words better than you can on your own, so grab someone else to listen. For example, be careful when utilizing the word *you*. It can imply some aggression on your behalf. "Oh, you believe that? Well, let me tell how things really were in the Bible."

Do you know anyone who claims they cannot trust the Bible because the ancient people were prone to believe in the supernatural? Commit them to prayer and ask God for an opportunity to speak with them about this matter.

Now let's consider a second dismissive response people sometimes give.

Reason #2. Smart people rely solely on scientific evidence for their beliefs. That is why religious people are unintelligent. They would rather have blind faith for which they have no scientific evidence.

To uncover the foundation of this argument, you may ask this question: What do you mean by that?

Short Response: This reason for calling Christians unintelligent is wrapped up in some assumptions.

Can you find any of the assumptions? Write them here:

On a quick glance, I notice two basic assumptions:
1) The person assumed that Christians want to blindly believe without any evidence or reason and therefore care little for the truthfulness of their own beliefs, and
2) They assumed that it is possible to have scientific evidence for everything a person believes.

You may have found some different assumptions from the ones I found, which is why having a group of fellow believers all committed to the truth and to effectively sharing the truth is so valuable. There's a lot wrapped up in this misconception.

Did you think of any other assumptions? Write them here:

Now try to write a statement demonstrating your knowledge of the scientific evidence for why you do that particular thing in the morning. Please cite any specific scientific studies you can name.

1.

2.

3.

4.

Once again, we have a statement that is overreaching. I'm sure some Christians do not care to reason or evidence what they believe. Just as surely some atheists behave likewise. The problem with this statement is that it refers to a human trait, not a trait of solely religious believers. Some people do not wish to spend the time to evidence and reason their beliefs. Yet, some people do desire to investigate whether or not their beliefs are true. The statement generalizes all Christians into one simplistic category, without considering that there are many different people in the Christian faith.

Further, the argument assumes that a person can provide scientific evidence for everything he or she believes. This is a grossly false statement. To scientifically prove every belief a person acts on—from the moment she awakes until the moment she falls asleep—would require more than one human lifetime.

Try to think of every decision you must make before leaving your home in the morning (for wherever you are going, such as church, work, school, shopping). List a few of them here:

1.

2.

3.

4.

You may have been able to write one or two things. You may have not been able to write anything at all. Whether you are an atheist or Christian, what should come to light is that the same problem remains: We cannot prove all the beliefs that we act on everyday (as mentioned in Week Two).

Think about that last statement. What does it mean that you cannot prove all the beliefs you act on everyday?

How could you use this statement in responding to the misconception that Christians are unintelligent? Be ready to share your ideas on this important matter.

A popular thought in our culture says everything we can know for sure is found in the methods of science (discussed in Week Four). This thought has become so pervasive that we are told to "leave our religion at church" or to "leave our religion at home."

The reasoning behind this thought assumes that religion is not provable by science and therefore does not inform us on anything at all. It's just your opinion uninformed by hard, scientific, defensible fact. However, there are scientific evidences for the existence of God. Further, religion informs us on issues that science cannot inform us—for example, the issues of ethics and philosophy of science.

A more realistic approach is to say that while we can know some things from scientific methods, there are other things we cannot know from any methods of science. The methods of science don't even have a way of verifying that the methods of science are accurately reporting information to us.

What is a question you could ask a person who believes that Christians are unintelligent?

What is a response you could give to a person who thinks Christians are unintelligent due to its pre-scientific origins?

What is a response you could give to a person who thinks Christians are unintelligent because they do not rely solely on scientific evidence for their beliefs?

CONFIDENCE BUILDER: In my writing, I tend to focus on evidence and reason within general revelation, including philosophy and history, as well as evidence and reason from special revelation with regard to theology and history. It is not my intention to discount the inner witness of the Holy Spirit as evidence and reason. His witness does count as evidence, but it is difficult for a skeptic to trust that evidence until she sees the outworking of that inner witness (dramatic life transformation, unusual love and kindness, etc). In watching lectures and debates of some of the world's leading Christian thinkers, William Lane Craig and John Lennox, I have noticed their concerted effort to discuss the validity of the Holy Spirit's inner witness. Their discussions on His witness are met with hostility and mockery at times, but the subject is an important and real part of the Christian faith, one that is often ignored and therefore misunderstood.

DAY THREE

CONVERSATION GOAL: To aptly respond to the argument that Christianity is based on a book of man-made myth

One very popular misconception in our culture is that the Bible is a man-made myth. In making this claim, the story of Jesus is compared to the story of pagan gods from Egypt and Greece, as well as gods from Persian religions. Critics claim that we no longer believe in any of these other gods, so no one should believe in Jesus.

The claim has gotten much attention from *New York Times* bestselling author and atheist, Richard Dawkins. It has also garnered celebrity support from comedian, Bill Maher on television, in his movie *Religulous*, and in his comedic routine on the road. A quick online search will pull up this as one of the top arguments against Christianity. I have even heard this argument made in a few formal debates between Muslims and Christians. It is a claim to which you may likely have to respond. So let's go to it!

What does 2 Peter 1:16-19 say about the origin of the message about Jesus?

What did Peter claim concerning the power and coming (second coming) of the Lord Jesus Christ?

According to 2 Peter 1:3-9, why does Peter make this claim? What is he concerned about?

Peter apparently ministered in an area where false teachers taught that the second coming of the Jesus was something similar to mythology. The believers, therefore, had begun to have doubts about their faith. So Peter reminds these believers to continue building themselves up in their faith (adding goodness, knowledge, self-control, endurance, godliness).

Peter states that these things confirm the reality of their belief in Jesus Christ and are ultimately grounded in the truth of His return. Why should they believe in the final resurrection at the return of Christ? Peter proclaims that he was an eyewitness to Christ's revelation of His majesty and glory, referencing the experience on the mount of transfiguration (Matt. 17:1-9). Peter emphasizes that he was not following after "cleverly devised myths," but that he actually witnessed this event himself (2 Pet. 1:16). He's concerned these believers may forget his testimony when he is no longer with them.

What is a myth? See if you can write out a definition.

Why do you think people say that Christianity is a man-made myth?

Have you ever responded to this claim? What did you say?

If you have never responded to this claim, what do you think you could say?

How might you phrase your response in the form of a question or series of questions?

In the passage we read, Peter utilizes the Greek word *mythos* to mean a man-made story, something made up. *The Baker New Testament Commentary* defines a myth as "a story which man has formulated to express his own desires without any reference to reality. Because of its man-centered focus, a myth is devoid of redemptive power."[2]

Peter directly contrasts man-made myth that has no power of redemption to his eyewitness testimony of the power of Jesus Christ. He is explicit and purposeful in his intent: This is no myth.

As other Jews in his day, Peter was well aware of the mythological gods worshipped all around them. The Jews, like Peter, abhorred these gods because he had been taught about the suffering of their forefathers due to idolatrous worship.

Peter and other early Christian leaders went to great lengths to prevent pagan worship practices from getting mixed with the worship of God. So this is no small matter to Peter, and he is not the only New Testament author to warn against myth. We also find Paul warning believers against wandering off into or following after myth in his two letters to Timothy.

Read 1 Timothy 1:4; 4:7; 2 Timothy 4:4. From these passages, what could you say in responding to the claim that the Bible is myth?

My response, so far, may look something like this:

> **Me:** Why do you believe the Bible is myth?

> **Person:** Over time people have believed many myths; the Bible is one of them.

> **Me:** The authors of the New Testament were aware of the myths in their day. They specifically expressed that they were not following cleverly devised myth, but saw Jesus for themselves. Further, they encourage, even command, that people not get caught up in myths. What reason do we have to distrust their warning against myths or to distrust their eyewitness testimony?

> **Person:** I'm not sure. However, they could have just made this stuff up.

Let's take a moment to answer the last statement. I was recently asked this question: How do I know that the authors didn't just make this stuff up?

Can you think of a way to respond? Write it here:

In John Lennox and David Gooding's work, *Christianity: Opium or Truth?*, I recently encountered a refutation of the man-made myth argument. The authors state, "The first thing to say about it would be, that if the character of Jesus is a literary fiction, then what we have here is a near-miracle. We know a lot about fictional literary characters and how difficult it is to create a really convincing one. World literature is full of such characters, some well drawn, some not so well. Now there is no denying that if Jesus is a literary fiction, he is a character that has achieved world-wide fame. To be able to create such a famous fictional character, the authors of the Gospels must have been literary geniuses of the highest order. Now literary geniuses of that rank are quite rare: one does not bump into one round every corner. But here we have four all flowering at once. Who were these men? And what kind of men were they? Well, two were fishermen, one was a low-level tax-official, and the other a non-descript young man. Is it credible that all four happened to be literary geniuses of world rank?"[3]

Jesus would be one of the greatest—arguably the greatest—created fictional character of all time. Think of the billions of people who have believed Jesus is the redeeming Savior of the world and how much Jesus' salvation has shaped and changed cultures all over the earth. Yet, "even the most brilliant, life-like fictional characters remain for their readers just that: fictional."[4] These characters do not rise up 'out of the pages' for people to become a living person with whom people believe they have a relationship. Think of such enduring characters as Shakespeare's Hamlet and Charles Dickens' Scrooge.

"If Jesus was in fact a fictional character invented by the authors of the Gospels, then in creating a character who for millions has become a living Person worthy of love, devotion and sacrifice, those authors have achieved a literary feat unparalleled in the whole of world literature. Miracle would not be too strong a word for it. Perhaps, indeed, we ought to start worshipping them [the authors]?"[5]

Can you name another character in literature whose story was created by multiple authors at the same time, with the same story, and has the enduring and culture-shaping qualities of Jesus? His culture-shaping qualities include: moral reform, introduction of the modern sciences, shaping of governing systems, value of equal opportunity for education, literacy.

I cannot name such a character. Even if you don't believe in the supernatural, what you would have here is something akin to a literary miracle. We have multiple letters written by different authors in the same time frame who all have "created" nearly the same work of literary genius. It never happened before Jesus and it has not happened since Jesus. Rather, than straining reason with a fictional character explanation, it makes sense to say that what we do have is multiple authors reporting the same impacting historical figure who lived in the area of Palestine during the reign of Tiberius Caesar.

Take a moment to write out, in your own words, a response to the myth theory using the argument from literature.

If you do speak with an atheist who has a degree in literature, how could you approach this topic, specifically if you do not have a degree in literature?

Remember that questions help you share responsibility rather than place all the responsibility on yourself. You don't have to always be the expert in the room. Sometimes, you allow the other person to be the expert. When I find I'm engaged with a person who has a degree in an area involving an argument for belief in God, I ask them something like: What do you think about this idea? Do you see any strengths or weakness to the argument?

How does the dynamic of conversations change if you allow the Holy Spirit to be in charge of results?

Think how much more free and genuine your encounters can be if you take the artificial pressure off. You can even enjoy letting the other person be the expert. Let them give you a free education. At the same time you may make a much more positive impression on them for the cause of Christ.

If you'd like to read more about this argument, Dr. John Lennox of Oxford University and Dr. David Gooding of Queen's University have written this argument in chapter two of *Christianity: Opium or Truth?*

Typically, I find that people are arguing the man-made myth theory based on two reasons:

#1. Humans wrote the story and therefore it is made-up and/or flawed.

#2. Jesus' story mimics other stories of god dying-and-rising from the dead.

We have already discussed a response to part of the first reason. There could be a lot more to unpack in that reason. You should find out what is the specific objection.

If the objection is stated that humans wrote down the story of Jesus and therefore it is flawed, what might you ask in response?

I always probe further into why a person thinks all human writing must be flawed. "What do you mean by that?" is the question I would ask. I typically point them towards understanding that most of what we know as individuals is by way of someone else's writing. Therefore, it seems too skeptical to distrust something because humans wrote it. To hold to that skepticism would be to blow up most of our knowledge.

The second reason revolves around the claim that Jesus' story is copied from other stories of ancient gods. To this claim, one should ask, "What is your source for those stories?" or "Where are you getting that from?"

Over the years of reading the stories of other gods, I have not found them to be the same. There are general similarities, such as existence of the supernatural, the desire for a savior of mankind, the practice of praying, the practice of ritual feasts, belief in resurrection (of some kind), and belief in a heaven and hell. However, the overall philosophy and the details of the stories are vastly different leading towards dissimilar morality, traditions, and cultures.

For example, people compare the worship of Jesus to the worship of the Egyptian god Osiris, whose followers have a festival celebrating Osiris' phallus! Jesus is also frequently compared to the Roman god, Mithras, who never dies. If a god doesn't die, he cannot resurrect from the dead. So you want to find out where the person has heard this misconception or what they have read to believe it is true. In my experience, I rarely find a person who has read the actual sources for their claims. Rather, they have read a modern Christ-myth author, instead of the sources. Encourage them to read the sources. Many of the stories are available free online.

What could you ask someone who tells you that the story of Jesus is a copy of the stories of other gods?

VERBAL GIFT CARD: "I could see some general similarities between Christianity and other religious beliefs, but a huge difference separates the actual stories and theology. The difference can be seen in the stories themselves and the dissimilar cultures that develop from these religions."

FOR FURTHER STUDY

Read the stories from the sources.

For the Greek/Roman gods: The Internet Classics Archive, *classics.mit.edu*

For the Egyptian gods, Osiris and Horus: Egyptian Book of the Dead, *www.africa.upenn.edu*

THE HUMAN INTELLECT IS QUITE CAPABLE OF INTERPRETING SIMILAR EXPERIENCES IN A SIMILAR WAY, WHETHER IT BE THE INTELLECT OF A GREEK OR AN INDIAN, WITHOUT ITS BEING NECESSARY TO SUPPOSE THAT SIMILARITY OF REACTION IS AN IRREFUTABLE PROOF OF BORROWING.[6]
—FREDERICK COPLESTON

CONFIDENCE BUILDER: John N. Oswalt, in his book *The Bible Among the Myths* defines myth by those stories that contain a specific philosophical understanding of the universe called, "continuity." As Oswalt describes, "Continuity is a philosophical principle that asserts that all things are continuous with each other. Thus I am one with the tree, not merely symbolically or spiritually, but actually. The tree is me; I am the tree. The same is true of every other entity in the universe, including deity. This means that the divine is materially as well as spiritually identical with the psycho-socio-physical universe that we know."[7]

In understanding the difference between the mythical and biblical literature he states that the philosophical principle of continuity is found in all great religious literatures of the world except the Israelite one and its three derivatives, Judaism, Christianity, and Islam. "Myth is best characterized by its common understanding of, and approach to, the world. Above everything else this approach involves continuity. Myth depends for its whole rationale on the idea that all things in the cosmos are continuous with each other."[8] The Christian world view differs greatly in its Trinitarian-monotheism which entails that the divine and the creation are separate from one another and are not continuous with each other. Oswalt believes the Bible has been included in the current popular definition of myth, not because it qualifies as mythological literature, but because of a cultural paradigm shift broadening the definition of the word, myth, to purposefully encompass broader spectrum of religious literature.

DAY FOUR

CONVERSATION GOAL: To aptly respond to the argument that Christians are hypocrites

Lately, I've been in physical therapy for some neck issues. I'm trying to fight off the onset of thoracic outlet syndrome. It's been a battle, but in the fight, I've gotten to know a great person: my physical therapist. During one visit, she asked me what I write about. She knew my neck and shoulder trouble were related to using a laptop. I shared with her that I write about having effective conversations on belief in God. She asked me how I got involved with that topic, which she found unusual. So I was able to tell her my story about growing up atheist, becoming a Christian, doubting what I believed, and coming back around to belief in God. In her response to my story, she shared that one reason she didn't go to church was because there were too many hypocrites in the church.

How do you respond when someone says, "The church is full of hypocrites"?

If you've never encountered this misconception, think of what you might say. Remember to consider good questions to ask.

While I teach apologetics and the use of arguments to make a case for belief in the Christian God, I often find that what keeps people from committing to Jesus Christ is not traditional arguments. Rather, it may be an argument from observation of Christians' actual lives or an argument from the perception of what Christian lives should be. Let's look at both today.

How does Peter say we are to live among people (the "Gentiles") in 1 Peter 2:11-17?

What reason does Peter cite for living this way?

According to verses 15-16, what are we supposed to do with our lives?

Peter focuses on our Christian responsibility to the people around us. The word *honorable* means to be worthy of respect as demonstrated through a life of integrity, fairness, honesty, and uprightness. The "strangers and temporary residents" wording has a two-part implication.

First, the world in which you live is not your final residence, so you shouldn't fully plunge into the lifestyles of the people around you. Rather, we are to be wise with how we engage in our culture, choosing our participation based on continuity with Christ's model and teaching.

Second, since this is a temporary residence, you are to act as an honorable guest. As you can see from the demands of an "honorable" life, this is no small task.

In responding to the hypocrisy charge, we should first take an honest look at our own life "among the

Gentiles." Christians can live in a way that is dishonorable and unreflective of the sacrificial love of God. When we live in such a way, we do not demonstrate the freedom from slavery to sin we have in Christ. Those around us, whether our immediate community or the broader culture, can see that while we proclaim freedom, we continue to be slaves with our words and actions: hypocrisy.

What are some ways we Christians bring the hypocrisy charge upon ourselves? Think of small ways and large ways.

One of the most prominent public ways that Christians bring the hypocrisy charge upon ourselves is by our behavior in politics. Christians sing praises to God with the same mouth they use to tear down political candidates. As James 3:9-10 says of our mouths:

WE PRAISE OUR LORD AND FATHER WITH IT, AND WE CURSE MEN WHO ARE MADE IN GOD'S LIKENESS WITH IT. PRAISING AND CURSING COME OUT OF THE SAME MOUTH. MY BROTHERS, THESE THINGS SHOULD NOT BE THIS WAY.

We are supposed to be wise with how we participate in our culture. Publicly tearing down candidates verbally or in writing is not living honorably among our people. It also has the adverse affect of showing Christians as hypocrites who bless and curse mankind.

How can Christians actively and effectively participate in the political realm without sacrificing their public witness to the truth of God?

Christians can show interest in the heated topics of discussion in our day, but we are to do so in a manner of goodness that, as 1 Peter 2 describes, would silence the ignorant ramblings of foolish people. We are not to match our culture's slanderous behavior; to do so is to enslave ourselves to sin.

Here's the real kicker: Peter wrote this letter to a group of persecuted Christians. These people were suffering for what they believed about God.

We are not only to live in an honorable way when it is easy and/or comfortable to do so, but in every situation. By "every situation," I mean even the small, mundane tasks of everyday life. We can also show ourselves as hypocrites by the way we act around our immediate friends and family.

In what ways can a person demonstrate hypocrisy with their family and friends?

More frequently, in my talks with church youth, I must address the hypocrisy of family members who say they believe in Christ but fail to demonstrate a sincere trust in Jesus in everyday matters. I believe this is one reason that our youth check out of church when they leave the home: They do not see a real disciple of Jesus modeled in their homes. When a person is all talk and no-show (or very little show), even kids can figure out the hypocrisy.

When I taught public school, we used to say, "Remember, more is caught than taught." In our homes and with our families, we are constantly learning from each other. What are you teaching about faith in Christ through your attitude and actions? Think of the even the smallest things, from complaining about the dishes to the way you look at your child/spouse/parent.

We want to make sure that as people who profess to follow Christ, we are the first to admit our failure to regularly do so. Let's not wait for others to figure this out about us. This is one way to respond to the charge of hypocrisy. Another way to respond is to point out that a standard of goodness is implied when using the argument of hypocrisy.

When someone tells me that the church is full of hypocrites, I ask a version of my all-too-familiar question, "What do you mean by that?" Typically, I'll get a response related to how Christians teach love and forgiveness, but they are the most unloving and unforgiving people. Sometimes I hear that Christians preach against all sorts of sin, yet Christians are constantly engaging in and struggling with all the same sins.

What would you say in response to "Christians are caught up in the very sins they preach against"? Plan to discuss responses with your group.

What does Paul say he wants to do in Romans 7:14-25?

What does Paul say he continues to do, even though he doesn't want to?

In verses 16, 22, and 25, Paul mentions a standard by which he knows what is good. What is that standard?

Paul describes a situation in this passage that helps us to understand hypocrisy in the life of Christian believers. He mentions that he knows the law of God, the spiritual law by which he knows what is good. However, he struggles with his own sin, creating a constant fight within him between knowing what is good and doing what is not good.

The law of God is a moral compass by which we understand goodness in a more concrete, practical way. When a non-Christian points out that a Christian is a hypocrite, the non-Christian is unknowingly in agreement with Paul's writing in Romans 7.

Further, notice that the non-Christian, in making the hypocrisy claim, uses God's law as the standard of goodness to which the Christian is being hypocritical. Why would a non-Christian who doesn't believe in the law of God use it as though it were a real thing to make their claim of hypocrisy? They should not use it. The only way a Christian can be a real hypocrite is if there is a real law of God they are violating. Rather than disproving the existence of God, the hypocrisy objection uses God's existence to make the objection.

Restate the problem with the hypocrisy objection and the law of God in your own words.

In an atheist view, there is no law of God. A Christian cannot violate something that does not exist. So it is illogical for an atheist to use hypocrisy as an argument against belief in God, when hypocrisy against God's law is only possible if God, and His moral law, exists.

Using the material above, what could you say to someone who states that Christians are a bunch of hypocrites, and that's why they do not believe in God? Practice saying your response out loud.

While practicing your responses, think of different ways this objection may be stated to you. Write them down here.

Final thought on this argument. What difference do you think humility on the part of the Christian witness makes in dealing with the hypocrite objection?

VERBAL GIFT CARD: "I agree that the church is full of hypocrites; that's because the church is full of people. Hypocrisy is a human trait that is not specific to religious believers. Anyone can be a hypocrite."

DAY FIVE

CONVERSATION GOAL:
To put into practice the responses to misconceptions about the Christian faith

Throughout this week, we've answered some heavy-hitting false beliefs about Christians and Christianity. Let's do some review.

Name three false beliefs about Christianity from this week's study:
1.

2.

3.

What are some first responses (specifically questions) that you can give when you hear or read one of these false beliefs?
1.

2.

3.

Give one response to each of three false beliefs we learned about this week:
1.

2.

3.

Now, let's put these responses into a mock dialog with a friend. Get a partner to play devil's advocate with you. They will be the person with the objection based on a misconception. You will be the Christian who is attempting to effectively and graciously respond.

Mock-Dialog Scenario #1: "I don't believe in Christianity, because it came from a pre-scientific era."

Mock-Dialog Scenario #2: "Christians are ignorant."

Mock-Dialog Scenario #3: "Christianity was made-up by a group of people who stole the basic story from other myths."

Mock-Dialog Scenario #4: "How do I know this stuff isn't just all made-up?"

Mock-Dialog Scenario #5: "Christians are a bunch of hypocrites."

As you practice with your partner, have them watch out for any emotionally charged wording as well as for your timbre and inflection. See the checklist below:

1. Does your timbre aptly reflect the meaning of your responses?

2. Do you sound condescending in any way?

3. Was there any inflection of words that could be taken negatively?

4. Are you demonstrating a true concern for the other person? In what way?

5. If you were the person making the claims above, would you feel respected and encouraged at the end of this mock dialog?

As you wrap up your mock dialog, don't forget to include some scenarios in which the person still adamantly disagrees with you. Think of something you can say that would still breathe words of life to them, even in disagreement. Our responsibility is to give praise, honor, and glory to the Lord, no matter to whom or in which situation we speak. We can do so by representing Christ's goodness even when we are in a conflicted conversation.

JESUS IS A COPY OF PAGAN MYTHS, PART ONE

Christianity met the mythological search for romance by being a story, and the philosophical search for truth by being a true story.[9]

A quick search online of Jesus and myth reveals a currently popular idea—that Jesus is a copy of the mythological gods, therefore Jesus doesn't exist. Perhaps you have heard the sound bite, "We are all atheists about most of the gods that humanity has ever believed in. Some of us just go one god further."[10] The argument that Jesus' actual existence was a myth dates back to 19th century theologian Bruno Bauer. This 19th century view has been regurgitated in numerous works since. However, as historical Jesus scholar Dennis Ingolfsland points out, "Bauer simply fails to deal with the evidence. There is simply too much historical evidence to deny Jesus' existence."[11]

Even highly critical scholars, such as those in the Jesus Seminar, are confident Jesus was a historical person.[12] John Dominic Crossan of the Jesus Seminar states in *Jesus: A Revolutionary Biography,* "That he was crucified is as sure as anything historical can ever be."[13] A closer look at the evidences will demonstrate why the Christ myth is rejected by the majority of scholars who study the New Testament documents.

The Accepted Facts

The Christ myth theory ignores the evidence available concerning the historical person of Jesus. Dr. Gary Habermas of Liberty University has studied and/or surveyed 3,400 sources published in French, German, and English on the historical Jesus.[14] Though these scholars range from atheist to theological conservative, Habermas found certain facts agreed upon by virtually all the critical scholars concerning the person of Jesus:

1. Jesus died by Roman crucifixion.
2. He was buried, most likely in a private tomb.
3. Soon afterward, the disciples were discouraged, bereaved, and despondent, having lost hope.
4. Jesus' tomb was found empty very soon after his interment.
5. The disciples had experiences they believed were actual appearances of the risen Jesus.
6. Due to these experiences, the disciples' lives were thoroughly transformed, even being willing to die for this belief.
7. The proclamation of the resurrection took place very early, at the beginning of church history.
8. The disciples' public testimony and preaching of the resurrection took place in the city of Jerusalem, where Jesus had been crucified and buried shortly before.
9. The gospel message centered on the death and resurrection of Jesus.
10. Sunday was the primary day for gathering and worshipping.

11. James, the brother of Jesus and a former skeptic, was converted when he saw the risen Jesus.

12. Just a few years later, Saul of Tarsus (Paul) became a Christian believer due to an experience that he believed was an appearance of the risen Jesus.

These facts contradict the idea that Jesus never existed. A doubter of Jesus' existence must ignore the majority of the critical scholarship about Jesus' life and side with the incredibly small scholarly minority. Keep in mind that the majority referred to above includes the atheist, skeptical, and theologically liberal scholars.

But Wait, There's More

The skeptic might argue that the facts concerning Jesus' existence are from one source only, the New Testament. But that makes two mistakes. First, the New Testament isn't just one source but a collection of twenty-seven letters (different sources) with some surviving manuscript copies dating back to the second century. Second, many sources outside of the biblical texts mention Jesus. Jesus is mentioned in Justin Martyr's *Dialogue with Trypho*, Flavius Josephus' *Antiquities 18.3*, Cornelius Tacitus' *Annals 15.44*, Lucian of Samosata's *The Death of Peregrine*, Mara Bar Serapion's *A Letter of Mara, Son of Serapion*, the Jewish Talmud in b. Sanhedrin 43 and b. Sanhedrin 107, Pliny the Younger in *Epistles 10.96-97*, Thallus' writing on the history of the Mediterranean c. A.D. 52 (through Julius Africanus' remarks concerning this work), C. Suetonius in *Claudius 25.4*, and later works of Judaism, such as the Jewish Toledoth (a parody of the Christian gospel story). Just from these outside sources, the following facts about Jesus can be known:

1. Jesus lived during the time of Tiberius Caesar.

2. He lived a virtuous life.

3. He was a wonder-worker.

4. He had a brother named James.

5. He was acclaimed to be the Messiah.

6. He was crucified under Pontius Pilate.

7. He was crucified on the eve of the Jewish Passover.

8. Darkness and an earthquake occurred when he died.

9. His disciples believed he rose from the dead.

10. His disciples were willing to die for their belief.

11. Christianity spread rapidly as far as Rome.

12. His disciples denied the Roman gods and worshipped Jesus as God.

Considering these Christian and non-Christian sources and what is known about Jesus from them, the argument that Jesus never existed is blatantly false. This is a diverse collection of outside source material that aligns with the twenty-seven New Testament documents and that demonstrates the existence of the biblical person of Jesus.

The Source Material

Skeptics pose another argument in an attempt to deny the reality of Jesus. They suggest that the sources are unreliable. But, when compared to source material for other ancient figures in history, the source material about Jesus is very reliable—mainly due to the quantity of sources available. Historian Paul Maier states, "Many facts from antiquity rest on just one ancient source, while two or three sources in agreement generally render the fact unimpeachable."[15] A vast number of sources attest to the person of Jesus.

Another argument surrounding the source material is that there are too few cross-references for verification of those extra-biblical documents. A closer look will reveal that this same criterion would make knowledge of nearly all ancient historical figures invalid. John Warwick Montgomery, Emeritus Professor of Law and Humanities, University of Luton, England states, "The New Testament documents must be regarded as reliable sources of information ... the documentary attestation for these records is so strong that a denial of their reliability carries with it total skepticism toward the history and literature of the classical world."[16] Due to the amount of information and scholarly work available about the extra-biblical sources for Jesus' existence, a consensus of the scholars would be necessary to build the case against Jesus' existence.

The argument that Jesus was a myth disregards the consensus of scholarship, and ignores the historical evidence. No other person in ancient history has more evidence for their life than Jesus Christ. In fact, British scholar Norman Anderson argues, "The basic difference between Christianity and the mysteries is the historic basis of one and the mythological character of the others. The deities of the mysteries were no more than 'nebulous figures of an imaginary past,' while the Christ whom the apostolic kerygma proclaimed had lived and died only a few years before the first New Testament documents were written."[17]

In Part Two, we'll look at how a Christian faced with the mythology argument can respond by taking three steps to answer the claim: 1) Read the stories for yourself, 2) Take the parallels head-to-head, and 3) Set everything in context.

6

ENGAGE IN TOTAL TRUTH

GROUP

KEY CONCEPTS THIS WEEK:
1) the sacred/secular split and how it affects Christians
2) letting go of the sacred/secular split for the sake of conversation with others
3) practicing the conversation skills in role-play situations

QUESTIONS FOR DISCUSSION:
1) What is the sacred/secular split?

2) Why is it vital that Christians let go of this split in their own lives?

3) If you haven't been living in freedom in the area of being a public Christian, what's been holding you back?

4) Why do you think Christians have such a difficult time living in freedom in our culture (in the area of conversation about God)?

5) What does Jesus mean by "if the Son sets you free, you really will be free" in John 8:36?

6) What are some practical ways to combat the untruths of our culture that influence our minds?

Free video session downloads available at *www.lifeway.com/LivingInTruth*

CALL TO ACTION:

Throughout our study, we've been learning to effectively converse on the matter of truth. We need to take our skills out for a test drive. What person in your life has been asking you difficult questions? Let's get engaged in that conversation. Who is the person in your life that makes derogatory statements about Christians or the Christian faith? It's up to you to ask "what do you mean by that?" Would you and your group take some time to pray that God would entrust you with a conversation on truth? Even think of specific people in your lives who need the freedom of salvation in Jesus Christ. As we close out our weeks together, here are some more posts to share. Remember to tag me. @maryjosharp #LivingInTruth

We have a mission of freedom to pursue: liberating minds from cultural dogma that stigmatizes conversation about God in the public square. #LivingInTruth

The hope of the world brings redemption to a decaying culture. #LivingInTruth @maryjosharp

You are a participant in God's salvific work in the world, sharing the reality of freedom in Christ. #LivingInTruth @maryjosharp

You need not be restrained or chained by the cultural untruths, such as "religion is a private matter." #LivingInTruth @maryjosharp

Christ's freedom means you are free to do good, to be Christian in all areas of your life. #LivingInTruth @maryjosharp

You are truly free in Christ, but unless you remain in His Word, you will begin to enslave yourself to cultural untruths. #LivingInTruth

Therefore, if the Son sets you free, you really will be free. John 8:36 #LivingInTruth

Our response to verbal abuse is to shine like stars in a misguided generation. Philippians 2:15 #LivingInTruth @maryjosharp

Christians have often utilized an old analogy to discuss their Christian life: the cruise ship versus the battleship. The cruise ship is designed for the passenger's ultimate comfort, while the battleship is designed for the passenger to engage in warfare. Each bears the burden of their purpose. The cruise ship is built for smooth sailing and has a difficult time with any tactical maneuvering. The battleship is built to handle an unexpected turn of events, purposefully advanced in tactical maneuvering.

Throughout our few weeks together, we've been slowly transferring from a comfortable daily cruise to a more raucous vessel of living in truth. It can be an uncomfortable ride, especially when our vessel makes a sudden turn, throwing off our daily routine, or when we come under attack. However, the reality is that we are in a battle, a battle for truth in a society where even conversation about truth is under attack. We need all hands on deck to help keep conversation alive.

In our final week together, we'll look at how our current culture desperately needs confident Christians who are actively living in the truth to redeem conversation.

Let's focus on getting started in conversing with others as part of actively living in the truth.

• • • • •

DAY ONE

CONVERSATION GOAL: To practice recognizing the sacred/secular split

In 1984, the Apple Corporation aired a George Orwell inspired commercial that rocked the Superbowl. In the commercial, drone-like, mindless-looking people dressed in grey filed into an auditorium, listening to the brainwashing mantra of Big Brother projecting on a wall-sized screen (the scene is based on Orwell's dystopian novel, *1984*). As they listen, a lone female athlete races up the center aisle in bright orange shorts carrying a sledgehammer. No one is moving, they stare zombie-like at the wall of dogma radiating from the screen. The intensity builds as the athlete approaches the screen. We see guards run towards her. Suddenly, she stops. With all her might, she begins to swing the hammer around and around. The guards move in closer, nearly upon her. With one last spin, she agonizingly releases the hammer into the screen, setting off an explosion of light, liberating the people's minds. She has broken the people free from the dogmatic mantra of their culture!

We, too, have a mission of freedom to pursue. Our task is to liberate minds from a cultural dogma that is stigmatizing conversation about God in the public square. What is the Big Brother idea constraining our society from discussing their views? We can describe it as the sacred/secular split.

This dogma wreaks havoc on public conversation about truth. It creates a society full of mantra-repeating people chanting, "Keep your religion out of _____(insert school, government, public venues, etc.)" And this mantra is more widespread than just emanating from atheists and atheist organizations.

In Nancy Pearcey's book *Total Truth: Liberating Christianity from Its Cultural Captivity*, she describes an increasing phenomenon in our minds in which we divide life into "a sacred realm, limited to things like worship and personal morality, over against a secular realm that includes science, politics, economics, and the rest of the public arena."[1]

In our society this split is reinforced by a broader division sociologists call the public/private split. Any institutions falling in the public sphere (the state, academia, large corporations) are said to be "scientific" based and "value-free." Any institution falling into the private sphere (family, church, and personal relationships) are said to be ascertained from personal choice, opinions.

What personal or societal problems do you think may arise by dividing life up into the sacred and the secular?

Pearcey states, "The result is that religion is not considered an objective truth to which we submit, but only a matter of personal taste which we choose."[2] In this system of thought, religion has nothing to offer in any public arena because it is not based in fact.

Worse yet, this split is found in the mind of Christians who compartmentalize their faith into a religious life and everyday life. We have not only fallen victim to but also adopted the sacred/secular split!

The division of life into the sacred and secular or public and private spheres has successfully kept Christians from including God in their everyday conversations. They fear that the sacred is a personal matter and it is rude (or possibly unethical) to discuss their sacred beliefs in public.

To what degree do you think you struggle with the sacred/secular split? Why?

Why is this split so devastating in the Christian life?

Do you think you've ever stopped yourself from having a conversation about God because of fear about violating the sacred/secular split, even if you didn't know that was the cause?

I've mentioned before that I had troubles talking to people about my belief in God in everyday life. I had bought into the cultural mantra of the sacred/secular split. I just didn't know that my thinking was a societal dogma, and struggled with whether or not my belief was true. Christians must reject this division of life into different spheres because it is "the greatest barrier to liberating the power of the gospel across the whole of culture today."[3]

To what does Jesus compare His followers in Matthew 5:13-16?

What do you think this comparison means?

In a familiar beatitude from the Sermon on the Mount, Jesus calls His followers to be salt in the world. While many things have been said about this passage, one thing truly stood out to me: salt combats deterioration.[4] Christians are those who combat destructive powers in our culture and in our world.

As we have seen, the cultural dogma of the sacred/secular split is one of those destructive powers. It causes Christians to back down from sharing freedom in Christ, from being the salt that combats deterioration. It closes the minds of the people, and creates a mental block that prevents the pursuit of truth. It is an enslaving view, which we must not allow to master any one of us. The driving mechanism of this view is fear.

What does Peter encourage believers not to do in 1 Peter 3:13-16?

What does he say we should do instead?

Why should we do this?

In this passage, Peter encourages a group of fearful believers who were suffering for their beliefs. Though scholars are uncertain as to the exact type of persecution—whether physical, verbal, or material—these intimidated believers feared to share what they believed about God.

Look at verse 15 again. Peter specifically comments that they should trust the Lordship of Christ by being ready to give an answer to anyone who asks a Christian for what he or she believes. Peter's view permits no split of the Christian life between the sacred and the secular. We are always to be ready to answer in any situation, at any time, in any place.

You have the hope of the world that brings redemption to a decaying culture. You are a participant in God's salvific work in the world, sharing the reality of freedom in Christ, liberating mankind from enslavement to sin.

Are you willing to sling the sledgehammer of truth at the cultural dogma of the sacred/secular split?

Which part of Peter's command do you need more help to stand up to the mantras of our day?
❏ courage to question and respond
❏ courtesy to respond with gentleness and respect
❏ both

Can you think of something you can do right now to help "liberate the gospel from its cultural captivity"? Try to think of small things you can do today, as well as larger life goals.

I'm asking you to shatter a cultural myth that keeps people in the dark. It is no easy task, for you will be questioned, criticized, and confronted. Yet, as Peter described, this is part of making Christ the Lord of your whole life.

Let's end today with prayer for the task before us.
1. **Pray for our culture and its destructive path towards untruth.**

2. **Pray for your fellow believers to be gentle, respectful, and strong in salting the earth with hope.**

3. **Pray for your own journey in this area. Acknowledge where you are and where you'd like to be.**

4. **Thank our Lord Jesus for what He's done and what He's going to do.**

DAY TWO

CONVERSATION GOAL: To release the sacred/secular split in our lives

Today, we reflect on our own situation with regard to living in truth. Have we really let go of the sacred/secular split and opened ourselves up to living in the freedom of Christ? This is one of those areas of life that is a lot easier said than done. Some Christians still struggle with thinking religion is strictly a private matter, so they shouldn't talk about their beliefs in public. We'll address this issue in three steps: 1) understanding Jesus' teaching on being set free, 2) applying Jesus' teaching to the sacred/secular split, and 3) creating a path forward to continue to converse in freedom.

STEP #1: UNDERSTANDING JESUS' TEACHING

What did Jesus say to the Jews who had become believers in John 8:31-32?

What do you think Jesus meant by "if the Son sets you free, you really will be free" in John 8:36?

John 8 began with the Pharisees arguing over the truthfulness of Jesus' witness in establishing His authority. The debate turns back to the subject of truth itself in John 8:30-36. Jesus makes a remarkable claim that causes the hearers—even those who believed in Him—to react with hostility. He says that if you make the Word of God the rule of your life, if you trust Jesus' authority as giver of truth, you are truly set free.

The hearers reacted with anger because, though they believed in Jesus, they also thought their position as Jews ensured that they had never been enslaved. Jesus responds by saying that anyone who continues in sin is a slave to sin. However, if anyone trusts in Jesus' authority to give freedom from sin, that person is actually free.

Commentaries explain this indicates the study of God's Word gives you genuine knowledge of the truth. "This knowledge, born of revelation and experience, sets one free."[5]

CONFIDENCE BUILDER: In John 8:30-36, Jesus addresses a group of Jewish believers who were offended because Jesus said they could be truly set free through Him. Do you see a parallel to this instance with modern society? Today many people believe they are free specifically because they do not follow any religious belief. They may be offended if you suggest that they are slaves to sin and need the freedom from sin that Jesus came to offer. On several occasions, people have told me that they do not like churches teaching about "sin" because it is offensive. Yet, if a person rejects this basic doctrine of slavery to sin, then he or she cannot be set free from sin.

C.S. Lewis wrote, "that we have used our free will to become very bad—is so well known that it hardly needs to be stated. But to bring this doctrine into real life in the minds of modern men, and even modern Christians, is very hard."[6] He further states, "Christianity now has to preach the diagnosis—in itself very bad news—before it can win a hearing for the cure."[7] We will have to teach about the reality of evil and sin in order for anyone to understand the need for freedom.

Only Jesus, as God, can give a person actual freedom, born out of genuine knowledge of the truth. By submitting to Jesus' authority as the giver of truth, I am releasing myself from the enslavement to deceptive philosophies (Col. 2:8) that result in false beliefs—such as the faulty view that Christians should keep their beliefs private.

If you are currently enslaved by this ideology, it can be difficult to get started in a conversation about belief in God. Yet, you need not be restrained or chained by cultural untruths, e.g., "religion is a private matter," "you're just shoving your religious beliefs on me," or "Christians are ignorant."

How does Jesus' claims in John 8:30-36 help release you from such cultural untruths?

How can you demonstrate that you trust in Jesus' authority on this matter, so you are truly free?

If you haven't been living in freedom in this area, what's been holding you back?

Christ's freedom means you are free to do what is good and true in all areas of your life, even in public conversations about God. For me, as an introvert, Christ's freedom means that I am not enslaved to my introver-

sion. I can have intellectually, emotionally, and spiritually satisfying conversations even with people I do not know. Christ's authority over all events and situations means I can trust Him even when I am fearful of what others will think of me in my workplace, community, or home.

Learning to live in Christ's truth isn't easy or immediate, but it is possible because of what He promised. The reality of the situation is that I can be set free, even in our society, to live as a Christian, as long as I continue in the Word of God, to actively grow in my knowledge of Him and relationship with Him.

STEP #2: APPLYING JESUS' TEACHING
We face a great challenge in moving from understanding Jesus' teaching on freedom to applying that freedom to our Christian lives.

Why do you think Christians have such a difficult time living in freedom in our culture? Focus on the freedom to speak about Christianity.

Many voices in our culture spread untruth about Christianity or stand in stark opposition to Christian truth. Think of just the messages communicated to us every day by television, movies, music, stores, campaigns, and advertisements—all using propagandist techniques to make us think in certain ways. It takes much time and energy to sift through so much visual and verbal communication noise to get to the root assumptions. Francis Bacon, an Enlightenment era champion of modern science, noted: "The trouble is this: things that strike the senses outweigh other things— more important ones—that don't immediately strike them. That is why people stop thinking at the point where their eyesight gives out, paying little or no attention to things that can't be seen."[8]

While Bacon's statement relates to discovering things we cannot immediately detect in nature (e.g., cells or microscopic organisms), think of how his statement applies to our thinking on difficult matters, such as the truth of God's Word, in the midst of all that communication noise.

How difficult do you find it to focus on truths from the Word of God during an average day?

1 ├────────────────────────────────┤ 6

Not Difficult   Very Difficult

What are some of the specific "noise-makers" that keep you from focusing in this life? If you do not find it difficult, explain why and what you are specifically doing to maintain focus. Plan to share answers with your group.

Daily tasks, cultural trends, and the news, especially political news, tend to grab up my immediate attention. When I have difficulty focusing on the Word of God, I also find it difficult to live in the freedom of Christ.

Look back at John 8:32. Jesus says those who continue in His Word are those who are free. You are truly free in Christ, but unless you remain in His Word, you will begin to enslave yourself to the cultural views.

How does remaining in God's Word directly apply to releasing us from the sacred/secular split?

When we remain in God's Word, learning the deep truths of who we really are as disciples of Jesus, we free ourselves to accept and follow true knowledge. We do not have to conform to our culture (Rom. 12:1-2). We are freed up to reject the pressures to conform to false knowledge and deceptive philosophies such as the sacred/secular split.

Christian author Nancy Pearcey comments, "Christians are called to resist the spirit of the world, yet that spirit changes constantly... to resist the spirit of the world, we must recognize the form it takes in our own day. Otherwise, we will fail to resist it, and indeed may even unconsciously absorb it ourselves. And yet haven't many of us done just that? Haven't many evangelicals shifted their beliefs to the upper story, holding them as subjective, personalized truth—"true for me" but not universally, objectively true?"[9]

Paul wrote to the church in Corinth. In a passage he wrote to help Christians live in Christ's freedom, he said, "Therefore, whether you eat or drink, or whatever you do, do everything for God's glory" (1 Cor. 10:31). Paul says everything we do is for God's glory, so no area of life is secular. That means no secular versus sacred truths. The truth that sets us free is to permeate our lives. But Jesus' command is easier to say than to enact.

What does it mean to say "no area of life is secular"? Do you agree or disagree? Plan to discuss with your group.

How does the sacred/secular split directly affect the Christian's ability to be Christian in public, such as in conversation about belief in God?

For me, the sacred/secular split shut down my public witness. It walled me up into a private Christianity that was mostly about me and for me. I hadn't become free to be a public Christian—unashamedly and naturally for the sake of others.

STEP #3: A PATH TO CONVERSE IN FREEDOM
What can you do today to apply your freedom in Christ to the sacred/secular split? Think of practical ways to effectively counter the spirit of the world constraining you as a public Christian. Note your thoughts.

You can begin by acknowledging and trusting that what Christ has declared, no society can reverse. This is one of the most important steps we can take in releasing the sacred/secular split.

We must do what James 1:27 commanded, "keep ourselves unstained from the world," in our thinking. "We tend to interpret that [James 1:27] in strictly moral terms—as an injunction not to sin. But it also

means to keep ourselves 'unstained' from the world's wrong ways of thinking, its faulty world views."[10]

Overcoming the sacred/secular split starts with our acknowledgement of faulty thinking. Our commitment to releasing the sacred/secular split will take a lifetime of combatting untruth in our culture. So you can find listed below some practical habits towards countering untruths. These are meant to give you some ideas, but not meant as a checklist of things to do. Choose one or two at a time so that you don't find yourself overwhelmed and giving up. Rather you want to invest in your scriptural and spiritual education:

- Find a Bible-reading routine that works for you (online plans for a week or a month or a year).
- Buy a one-year Bible that you read each day.
- Set regular alarms on your phone/laptop/tablet to alert you to read and pray (that one's for me!).
- Subscribe to a once-a-day dose of scriptural truth from a Christian website.
- Go through a study on basic Christian doctrines.
- Go through a study on basic apologetics.
- Get a daily prayer book.
- Don't feel guilty for taking time to pour into your spiritual life.
- Try not to rush through your reading.
- Never condemn yourself for missing a reading. This is an investment towards your freedom to converse, not an activity to burden you with just more things to do.

By investing in your education, you can begin to combat the untruths that come at you on a daily basis. Here are some of my direct thought patterns I use for combatting untruth. I try to regularly:

- Analyze the things I see and hear on a regular basis.
- Repeat to myself what I just saw or heard: for example, "The cosmetic commercial told me I would feel beautiful if I used their product."
- Ask myself, *what is the underlying assumption?*

(That I do not already feel beautiful with a further assumption that I am not beautiful without their product.)

- Ask myself, *does this assumption match the truth of God's Word?* (In the above case, no, it does not.)
- How do you know that it does or does not? (See 1 Sam. 16:7.)
- Determine what should I do with this communication? (In my example, reject the underlying assumption of this commercial as an untruth, also acknowledge the manipulative tactic to get me to buy something.)

Practice some "freedom thinking" with a partner. Use these scenarios:

- You're watching a favorite television show that just stated that Christianity is an ancient superstition that is outdated.
- You just saw an auto billboard advertisement with an image of a young, physically fit, attractive couple standing next to an expensive sports car. The text on the board said, "Only those who dare … truly live."[11]
- You just saw a movie in which the Christian characters were portrayed as spiteful, vindictive, and hypocritical.

Note some of your observations regarding the examples above.

These habits aid in tearing down the sacred/secular split in our lives and further help us to gain the confidence to speak with people anywhere at anytime. As Ken Sande states in his book, *The Peacemaker*, we cannot consistently weave the gospel into our conversations with others until the gospel is woven deeply into our own hearts.[12]

DAY THREE

CONVERSATIONAL GOAL: To learn to use questions to address the sacred/secular split

Now that we've studied the sacred/secular split, let's begin to question others who believe in this ideology.

Imagine your friend read an article in which a congressmen quoted the Bible as part of making a case for his view on a piece of legislation. She's really upset about him doing so and says to you, "I wish people would learn to keep their religion out of Washington!"

What could you ask her in response to her statement?

As per my typical response, let's say you ask, "What do you mean by that?" and she answers, "People should keep their religious views at home; that stuff is private. It shouldn't be brought up when it comes to making public policy."

Now what would you say?

I'm inclined to ask her, "Why do you believe that?" Remember, this split view of life is a cultural dogma. People need to be pressed to think about why they believe this view is true.

She now responds with, "This is just the way all reasonable people think." She is promoting her own view as unbiased and rational—suitable for the public square—while denouncing religious views as biased or prejudiced—unsuitable for the public square.[13]

What would you say in response to "This is just the way all reasonable people think"?

Let's think about that statement for a moment: "All reasonable people" means that to be considered "reasonable" one must agree with her. That doesn't sound very reasonable, does it? At this point, I'm inclined to ask her if she means that the Christian congressman should not be a Christian man when he is offering moral reasoning for a piece of legislation.

I'm in favor of turning this type of reasoning around on the person, not to create a flashy zinger, but to help them see the faulty reasoning. Should we demand that the atheist leave her world view at the door of her home and keep her beliefs private in the same situation? This request is impossible. A person's world view informs her whole life. It is her philosophy and her basis for morality. It is entirely appropriate to use your basis for morality when offering moral reasoning for a piece of legislation.

Why is it unreasonable to ask of a Christian, or atheist, to leave her "religion" or her "world view" at home?

Why do you think people say things like "leave your religion at home; it is private"?

Christians currently face much cultural pressure to leave their religion at home. However, the request is irrational. Christianity is a world view, so are atheism, Buddhism, Islam, etc. No way exists for people to leave their world view behind when they go somewhere. The idea is akin to asking a person to leave their mind at home. This unreasonable request is a result of the sacred/secular or private/public split. Let's look a little bit more at the origin of the split.

The sacred/secular split view comes most definitively from Enlightenment era philosophy concerning human reason.

Centuries prior to the Enlightenment, it was still held that human reason needed to be checked against the truth of God's revelation, which was used as a yardstick to discern untruth or error. However, even as early as the 1300s, reason was beginning to take on a more authoritative role than revelation in discerning true knowledge (see "Upstairs/Downstairs: the Sacred/Secular Split).

The work of philosophers such as Rene Descartes helped to establish a view of human reasoning that went beyond considering reason as the human ability to think rationally. Instead philosophers began seeing reason as an "infallible and autonomous source of truth" independent of religion or philosophy. Thus, reason became the replacement for God as the source of absolute truth.[14]

In the previous paragraph, underline the two different views of human reason, prior to the Enlightenment and post-Enlightenment

What problems do you see resulting from replacing God with human reason as the "storehouse of truth"?

What do you believe? Are there any facts to be found in your view of God? How do you know that?

We humans know that our reason is susceptible to error—great error. But if our reasoning ability becomes the sole basis or standard for truth, how could we ever know if we have any truth without error? We could not know. We need a standard for truth outside of humans that we use to compare our thoughts against. Our reasoning ability is a tool or a guide, but it is not infallible.

If your friend believes in the post-Enlightenment view of reason as an "infallible and autonomous source of truth" independent of religion or philosophy, she is prone to think that anything you say about religion or philosophy is just your biased opinion. Further, she may have no idea why she thinks this is so. Her view that religion is entirely subjective is why she is angry about the Bible quotation by the Congressmen. She wants hard, non-biased, objective facts—or so she may think.

When I say that salvation is found in Jesus Christ alone, I mean to share an objective truth—telling it like it is—a hard, non-biased, objective fact. I'm not just sharing my preference, something purely subjective. I base my belief on evidence of, reason for, and experience with God that has led me to trust Him and leads me on to trust Him more.

People have a difficult time with the truth claim about Jesus as the Savior for many reasons. But we've learned throughout our weeks together to question and respond to that distrust. Rather than opposing them, we can help them to work through their own objections. We need to first help them identify the basis for their ideas and then evaluate those reasons.

If, as I believe, salvation is found in Jesus Christ alone, then He certainly has much to say to us in the public square. We, as Christians, must utilize our belief in God to inform our daily lives in the public portions of our existence just as in the private.

What do you think people mean when they contrast what they consider facts to religious beliefs?

According to Isaiah 59:14, where truth is missing from the public square, what also is missing?

Why do you think some people believe no facts exist in religious views?

When truth is missing from the public square, what happens to those who turn from evil?

Wherever truth is missing, so goes honesty and justice. Wherever truth is missing, the righteous become prey to evil. Even Solomon noted the lack of goodness as he looked out over the land and saw evil where righteousness should have been (Eccl. 3). God's followers are supposed to be salt bearers of truth. We are to hold back the deterioration of our societies.

To posit divine truth is not an arrogant claim; it is a truth claim. We are not the only ones capable of knowing truth (Rom. 1), but we are commanded to share truth with our world. If a society declares that no truth exists, those willing to stand for truth become a prey. Christians, this is what happens as a result of the rebellion of mankind towards God. It should not catch you by surprise, nor should it cause you to give up being a public Christian.

What other response could you make to, "This is just the way all reasonable people think," now that you know a little of where she's getting this view? Or would you use the same response as you did previously?

Instead of a long discourse on the Enlightenment, Christians can question the Enlightenment view of reason by asking, "How do you know that?" You want to help her examine how she came to conclude that a reasonable human must accept her point-of-view. Be ready to be gracious and to use her response as a catalyst for learning together. This is not the time to tear people down for their beliefs, nor to get defensive. It is a time to bring healing to as many people in our land as possible.

To close out today, pray for:

1. an understanding of the sacred/secular split

2. a realization of how even Christians have allowed the sacred/secular split, based in "the deceptive philosophies of man" to lead our society away from truth and goodness

3. a commitment to live, as much as possible, in total truth with no split mind on life

4. for God to bring many people into your life with whom you can converse on truth.

VERBAL GIFT CARD: "I am a Christian and my view of God informs my view of life. It's not something I can leave behind me at home, since it is who I am. I expect that people who hold to differing beliefs from mine also cannot leave their views at home, for the same reason."

CONVERSATION GOAL: To learn to begin conversations on truth by following three actions

Some time ago, I was reading a list of "life hacks." These "hacks" are basically helpful hints for everyday situations. One of the hacks caught my attention: If you want to keep a pot of water from boiling over, place a wooden spoon across the top of your pot.

I have on many occasions let a pot of water boil over, as I am easily distracted while cooking. So this hack would be a blessing for me, but I was fairly skeptical that it would work. Still, I fired up the stove, put on a pot of water, and waited for it to boil. Once the boil began rolling pretty hard, instead of turning the heat way down, I turned it down slightly, placed a wooden spoon on top, and watched. Though the water churned with increasing intensity, it never boiled over the pot!

We've studied a lot of material over the last five weeks. All this information can make you feel like a pot ready to boil over. So today I'm offering you a life hack for having more effective conversation on truth: three steps you can take to begin conversing right away.

#1. Be alert.

#2. Practice questioning.

#3. Take the plunge.

#1. BE ALERT

I'm an overthinker, daydreamer, and an introvert. These qualities in me are a recipe for alertness disaster. For example, on numerous occasions my husband has caught me straying off into "the land in my head" when he was trying to tell me something.

Even with all the stories I tell about conversations with others, at times I fail to see anything other than that which I'm focused on. I'm actually surprised that I don't regularly run into a column, a wall, or another person. Often, I am reworking a reaction to a conflict or situation over and over in my head or I'm just having a moment in which I don't want to talk to anyone.

Without chastising myself for the times when I wasn't alert, I generally try to remember that I never know when an opportunity will present itself for a great conversation. I need to be open to God's work in others, in me, and in the world.

Do you have trouble with seeing the bigger picture (or seeing God's work) in an average day?

Do you often find yourself consumed with your reactions, emotions, and thoughts, inattentive to your surroundings?

On a scale from 1-6, how open would you say you are to conversation opportunities? 1 being almost closed off and clueless to 6 being willing and alert

1 ├──────────────────────────┤ 6

Read the following passages and note the main idea from each:

1 Peter 1:13

1 Thessalonians 5:6

James 1:22-25

Here's a few basic steps you can take towards alertness to your surroundings:

1. Challenge yourself to watch people.

2. Look for things about others that you find important.

3. Think of several background reasons for why a person may be in his or her current situation.

4. Compose some questions you might ask the different individuals you see.

When I people watch—or when I'm just looking around—I often find other people looking around. I have found that not everyone is looking down at phones, tablets, or computers these days (though sometimes I still do). Sometimes, when I make eye contact, they look away or just nod and smile, acknowledging me, but not wanting to talk. Other times, the eye contact operates as an invitation to converse. I then look for non-verbal cues to discuss.

Now, let's pretend that one of the people in your surroundings has given you an opportunity for conversation. This leads us into our second action after being alert.

#2. PRACTICE QUESTIONING

At my events, people have asked me how I get into conversations. I recently asked my daughter, "From your perspective, how do I generally get into a conversation about belief in God?" She replied, "Honestly, people just want to talk with you." She then added, "But, then there's Dad, and honestly, he just wants to talk with everyone!"

I'm really not a bona fide conversation-starter, but my husband definitely is one. Don't feel like you need to force a conversation to happen. Instead, be willing and ready to converse as God entrusts you with other souls. Part of being ready entails having some questions in mind that you typically ask people to engage them in conversation. So I'm going to offer some different kinds of scenarios that my family has encountered over the years in order for you to practice the questions from Week Four. Consider, as you practice, that it may take several questions to get to a question about religious beliefs or philosophy or God. Think of questions you might use to authentically interact in these situations.

AIRPORT

The person next you strikes up a conversation with you about your upcoming flight. It is delayed and they are lamenting/complaining about the delay. You notice the person has a thick foreign accent.

What could you ask or say to this person to engage in conversation?

My daughter and I discussed our usual responses and questions. We discovered that we'd probably say something like, "I have to give this kind of stuff over to God or I'd go crazy." Then I'd probably follow up with "Where are you from?" I'd then let a conversation happen naturally.

Sometimes, God will entrust me with a person who will say, "God ... ha! I gave up on God years ago." Sometimes, God will entrust me with a person who will say, "I'm from India/Pakistan/the Philippines/Australia/Wisconsin." I get all kinds of responses.

What would you ask next in both situations?

Write out one more response you might receive and then another question you could ask.

We will do some role-play in the "take the plunge" section, but you can also use these practice scenarios with a partner for role-play. Try re-starting the conversation with new responses, for example, responses that are further away from God-talk and responses that are closer to God-talk.

If you don't have a natural way of introducing a question about belief, don't rack your brains to dig up something. Personal questions, such as belief in God, may take building a safe conversation environment. Though you may strive to create that safe communication space, the other person may not be open to it. I have found sometimes conversation on belief happens right away, sometimes it happens slowly, and sometimes it doesn't happen at all. The point is to be ready for a conversation at any time—especially when you least expect it. In my experience, I typically get into conversations when I feel that I cannot do so because I'm sick or upset or sad. Let's look at another scenario.

BOOKSTORE

You are in a bookstore. You're currently browsing one section when you see the person near you has an overtly atheist book, for example, *Why I Am Not a Christian*, by Bertrand Russell. The person looks over your way and seems very approachable.

What could you ask to begin a conversation?

I'd most likely ask, "That looks like an interesting book. What is it about? It looks like it's about why the author left Christianity or why he doesn't believe in God."

What are some responses you are likely to receive? Some possible responses: "Oh, the book is about the argument for atheism," or "I don't really know but I'm kind of interested in what he has to say," or "Russell is an atheist philosopher who was partly responsible for the move away from God in our culture. He's one the important players in the 'God is Dead' movement."

What could you ask next? Continue to play out the conversation with a partner.

Here are some more places to create practice scenarios for your questions:

• Grocery Store
• Restaurant
• Department Store (I get into a surprising amount of God conversations when shopping for clothes or shoes.)
• Sports practice and/or game
• Church

Remember to work in clarifying questions, such as: *What do you mean by that? How do you know that?* and *Why do believe that?* Also, think about some places where you generally don't have conversation about God; pray that God would provide you opportunities in those places. For more practice with questioning, you can use Week Four in the study, *Why Do You Believe That?*

SIDE NOTE FOR CONVERSATION SETTINGS:
Remember some people are required to engage you because of customer service training. In these situations, please be discerning as to if the person really desires to talk with you about God and if he or she really has the time to do so. Other customers may also need to be served. The person may not be interested in your conversation. Don't try to force a conversation about God. The Lord is in control and He can use any conversation or situation for His glory.

My purpose for practicing questions is not to bamboozle people into talking with me about God but to create a safe environment for that conversation to unfold, should it do so. Since we don't have a God's-eye-view of the world, we don't know what is going on in each individual's life with whom we come into contact. Therefore, we should try to remain open to any situation that offers the opportunity to discuss belief in God.

Having let go of the sacred/secular split, I don't compartmentalize faith into certain days of the week or places of worship. Rather, I try to stay ready to live out Christian service and love to my fellow man anywhere, anytime. It's difficult sometimes because I don't always feel like doing so. And there really isn't a one-size-fits-all way to engage people in conversation. But I've noticed over the years that having good conversation has a lot to do with a willingness of heart to serve others (Phil. 2:3-4).

Would you be willing to commit to paying more attention to your environment for getting a conversation started?

If you're not there yet, consider what might be holding you back. God is aware of our struggles. If all you can do today is to say that you'd like to be more open to conversation, but you're not there yet, then say just that. There are many reasons for why a person doesn't want to have a conversation or doesn't feel ready to do so. Yet don't let your situation stagnate. As soon as you can, take the plunge into conversation.

#3. TAKE THE PLUNGE

Our daily life presents opportunities to have great conversations about truth with even our friends and family. You may hear a family member say, "Church is for idiots," or "I don't believe in God," or "The Bible is full of errors." These are open doors for discovering the basis of that person's belief. We are prone to see these statements as verbal attacks or rebellion—which they may or may not be. Either way, we can use these statements to minister to people who have said them, if we are willing to jump in (and if they are willing, too).

Find a partner and practice engaging in a conversation about the truth of the statements below. Your partner needs to be the person who makes the original statement objecting to the Christian faith unless you are in a group study, then you should take turns being the objector.

Remember that your purpose is not to win the argument. Your purpose is to assist the other person to examine his or her own beliefs. View yourself as an assistant rather than an opponent.

As each person takes a turn, try to make your conversation as realistic as possible. So try to think of what the objector to Christianity might actually say. The responder should try to discover the basis for the objector's belief. You can always use questions like, "How do you know that?" and "From where are you getting that?" "How did you come to that conclusion."

- Church is for idiots.
- I don't believe in God.
- The Bible is full of errors.

Now, write a statement that you've heard against the Christian faith.

Practice engaging in conversation with your original partner on this one. Remember to avoid negatively charged wording, use appropriate timbre, and to use inflection that accurately conveys your meaning.

Conversation is best learned by practice. The more you engage in conversation, the better you will become at conversation. Our goal is to more effectively minister to others—to speak the truth in love (Eph. 4:15). This is no easy task. Yet, it is worth the effort. When we open ourselves to minister to others through conversation, we begin to grow in our own faith.

Others will challenge us and make us think about our beliefs and how we know them to be true. That challenge is a good thing for Christians, especially in a culture that pushes the mantra that Christians don't want to think for themselves.

CONFIDENCE BUILDER: That more Christians begin to discuss truth with others is vital. We need to consider how we know what we know, and if we can know anything at all. I've noticed in my university courses that students—Christian students—are having a difficult time with the concept of true knowledge about anything. In one exercise in my logic class, I'll have students attempt to write the response to "what is a human?" They struggle with this exercise. The concept that something can be objectively true about human beings is so corrupted in our society that some of these students don't know if there's anything they can write to define a human. When they push back saying that the assignment is too subjective, I remind them that the debates on abortion, slavery, sex trafficking, human rights, and euthanasia all center on defining what is a human being.

One student argued that a human must be conscious and capable of rational thought, therefore if a "human" is in a coma, they are no longer human and could be put to death. I explained to her that her reasoning for what constituted a human (conscious and capable of rational thought) would exclude anyone who was sleeping. Therefore, by her definition of a human, I would have no moral obligation to let her live when she falls asleep. So I encouraged her to stay awake throughout my course (a little snarky logic humor)!

As you open up to having more conversations, you will notice that sometimes you have a great conversation you feel was productive. Other times, you have a conversation that doesn't go well and you might feel that you failed. I have many experiences with both situations. Sometimes, I just don't answer well or I forget to really serve the other person, or the other person really doesn't want to talk with me or they are hostile to Christianity. You can learn from any situation and from any conversation. The goal is to be willing and able to serve others in any circumstance out of love and respect for our fellow mankind.

CONVERSATION GOAL: To commit to living in truth for the sake of others

In 1985, the Apple Corporation aired a follow-up commercial to its groundbreaking ad from 1984. The commercial was titled, "Lemmings," and it depicted dark-suited business men and women mindlessly following each other in a line, blindfolded, and whistling "Heigh-ho, Heigh-ho, it's off to work we go." As the camera pulls back, we see more of the gloomy picture of these business people, not just marching to the humdrum of daily work life, but that they are marching off a cliff to their death in the abyss below. It's a disturbing picture. We then hear a voice-over introducing the Macintosh Office software, which catches the attention of one of the "lemmings." He removes his blindfold and avoids his destruction in the abyss.

This commercial was a huge disaster for Apple (compounded by the unmet promise of this product). The company took a major hit in sales causing layoffs and the firing of founder, Steve Jobs. What went wrong?

In the 1984 commercial, the hopeful athlete swung her sledgehammer of truth liberating the audience from the cultural mantra of "Big Brother." It was heroic and inspiring. In the 1985 advertisement, the "lemmings" trudging along had no hero, no inspiration, and the audience actually felt as though the Apple Corporation was attacking them personally, likening these potential buyers to lemmings if they didn't purchase the Apple product.

What lesson for sharing conversations about truth could you draw from the two Apple ads?

Throughout our time together, we've been learning to have confident conversations about truth. Truth conversations in our culture are difficult. Tensions are high. People may be confused about the topic.

We must make it our goal to speak the redemption and goodness of Jesus' truth into our culture. We are not here to call out people out as lemmings, nor to boost our own egos as liberators. That endeavor would be as fatally flawed as Apple's commercial.

Let's turn this thing around. You are me, seeking to teach good truth conversation skills.

How can we avoid, in our conversations, the Apple Corporation's mistake of insulting the audience whom they were trying to inspire?

How can we avoid using the conversation to boost our own egos?

The people with whom we hope to have conversations are sojourners with us on the earth in this time of God's salvation history. We are here to serve others by breaking through cultural mantra so that we may all live in truth (1 Tim. 2:1-4).

In our last day together, let's review the past weeks and think about the most impacting aspects of what we've learned.

WEEK ONE

What is truth (how did you define it)?

Why does truth matter to the Christian?

Why should we discuss truth with others?

WEEK TWO

What does it take for you to trust someone as an authority?

Is Jesus a trustworthy authority? Why?

Is there anything holding you back from trusting the one who laid down his life for you?

How do you wisely invest God's gift of the Gospel in others? Or are you doing so?

Do you trust Jesus to care for you as you risk investment in conversation with others?

WEEK THREE

What are five practical steps to engage in appropriate listening?

#1.

#2.

#3.

#4.

#5.

What is an objective statement?

What is a question you could ask about the statement, "Christians are intolerant"?

What is a subjective statement?

WEEK FIVE

What are emotionally charged words and how do they affect your conversation?

Why is it important to know the difference between subjective and objective statements when you are conversing about the truth of Jesus Christ?

What is one way you can respond to the claim that Christians are unintelligent?

6

WEEK FOUR

Why is it good to ask questions before responding to statements about belief in God?

What is one way you can respond to the claim that Christianity is a man-made myth?

What is a question you could ask about the statement, "Science is the only way to know truth"?

What is one way you can respond to the claim that Christians are hypocrites?

What is a question you could ask about the statement, "To be good, we don't need God"?

WEEK SIX

What is the sacred/secular split?

What can you do to help our culture break through this dogma to see truth?

How can you get started conversing with people right away?

We have an opportunity to shatter false ideas that may keep people from ever considering the truth of Jesus Christ. We can help our culture not slip into faulty thinking developed by following the dogma of our day rather than by serious inquiry into truth. This is a risk worth taking, a battle worth fighting, and a conversation worth having!

JESUS IS A COPY OF
PAGAN MYTHS, PART TWO

As mentioned in Part One, an increasing trend in popular and academic circles is to propose that the story of Jesus is a mythical one, copied from the stories of pagan mystery gods such as Osiris and Mithras. Not only can the claim be found on numerous internet sites and in several popular-level books, but it is also propagated by celebrities such as political satirist, Bill Maher.[15] On a September 2008 episode of the widely-viewed talk show, The View, Maher stated that the story of Jesus is exactly the same as the story of the Egyptian god, Horus. Do these claims have much merit? In the brief space to follow, I will focus on a method for investigating the stories of the other gods and the story of Jesus.

A METHOD FOR INVESTIGATION

#1. READ THE STORIES FOR YOURSELF

When faced with the question of whether or not the story of Jesus is a copy of another god's story, you should actually read the stories. Get a hold of a copy of the Egyptian Book of the Dead or the Hindu Bhagavad Gita and go through the stories for yourself (local college library, some city libraries, online texts). It's always a good idea to go to the primary source material so you know the subject being discussed from the source of the discussion.

#2. TAKE THE PARALLELS HEAD-TO-HEAD

After reading the stories, investigate the suggested parallel material from those stories. If someone claims that Horus had a virgin birth just like Jesus, see if you can find any virgin birth story in a primary source that mirrors the one of Jesus. In Horus' case, his birth has a few different stories depending on the different Egyptian dynasty sources. In one story, Horus' conception by the gods Osiris and Isis (brother and sister) occurs while these gods were still fetuses in their goddess mother's womb (these god-fetuses had intercourse in their mother's womb). In another story, Horus grows rapidly in his mother's womb and tears out of it.

Vague similarities are not going to accomplish much for those who are seeking to be in-tellectually honest. Continuing with the virgin birth theme, Mithras was "born of a virgin" and Jesus was "born of a virgin" is either too vague or is so strained as to be construed as dishonest reportage.[16] Mithras sprung forth from a rock (or cave) near a river bank. He was holding a torch to illumine the underworld from which he came and a dagger to subdue all the creatures of the earth. Jesus was born as a human baby by a female human virgin. In an-other version, Egyptian god, Osiris, was the product of an adulterous affair between two gods. He fell in love with his sister and had sexual intercourse with her in the womb of his mother goddess. The only thing similar in these virgin birth stories of Jesus, Horus, and Mithras is the vague similarity of birth itself.

#3. SET EVERYTHING IN CONTEXT

Some contemporary Christ-myth theorists will use terms like "resurrection" with stories of any god that died and took an afterlife form. For example, Peter Joseph used "resurrection" to fit his purpose of a side-by-side comparison of several gods in *Zeitgeist, the Movie*. Yet, did the people who followed the various gods understand their god to be "resurrected" in the sense of Jesus' resurrection? No. Jesus' resurrection was an unexpected twist in the Jewish view of the Messiah, as well as in the Jewish view of resurrection. It was also unexpected according to the pagan understanding of the afterlife; for Jesus was raised to a new, physical body. The pagans expected a spiritual union with their gods in the afterlife or a freeing of the spirit from bodily imprisonment. The unexpectedness of the resurrection of Jesus that Paul taught caused the pagan philosophers in Athens to ask, "May we learn about this new teaching you're speaking of? For what you say sounds strange to us, and we want to know what these ideas mean." (Acts 17: 19-20; see also vv. 16-18) This twist is important, because it has everything to do with the Christian understanding of God's good creation, His forgiveness, and His gift of salvation.

Jesus' resurrection stands unparalleled in history when attempting to find stories in which God purposed to pay the penalty for all of mankind's sin so that man can have a new, redeemed life. Jesus died as He expected and predicted, and for the purpose He planned. Even if a person does not believe in God, he can see this difference between Jesus' story and the story of the other gods. Jesus' resurrection is also the model for the resurrection of all of mankind. He is "the firstborn of the resurrection." The followers of Jesus in the first century up to today have a radically different view of the afterlife and resurrection from their fellow mankind. This is not something that can easily be overlooked in order to make an accusation of copying from other gods' stories. And we have just begun to dig into the differences!

CONCLUSION

Just like you and I do not want to have our ideas and words ripped out of context and used for someone else's purposes, we should not take the stories of the ancient gods and of the major world religions out of context to use for our own purposes. Nor should we be ignoring aspects of the stories that show their vast differences. The deeper we look into the stories of the gods, the greater the difference we find between them and the story of Jesus.[17]

A FEW OF THE RESOURCES UTILIZED:

Ronald Nash, *The Gospel and the Greeks* (Phillipsburg, PA: P&R Publishing, 2003).

T.N.D. Mettinger, *The Riddle of Resurrection: Dying and Rising Gods in the Ancient Near East* (Stockholm: Almqvist & Wiksell, 2001).

Joseph Campbell, *The Mythic Image* (Princeton, NJ: Princeton University Press, 1974).

N.T. Wright, *The Resurrection of the Son of God*, (Minneapolis: Fortress, 2003).

Bruce M. Metzger, *Historical and Literary Studies: Pagan, Jewish, and Christian* [online article]; Internet; available from *www.frontline-apologetics.com/religions_christianity.html*; accessed 22 January 2007; *Historical and Literary Studies: Pagan, Jewish, and Christian*. Grand Rapids: William B. Eerdmans Publishing Co., 1968.

PRIMARY SOURCE MATERIAL:

Hellenistic Religions: The Age of Syncretism, ed. Frederick C. Grant (Indianapolis: Liberal Arts Press, 1953)

The Egyptian Book of the Dead, trans. E.A. Wallis Budge (New York: Barnes & Noble, 2005 [1895]).

Christian Classics Ethereal Library Website: *www.ccel.org/*

Fordham University's Full Text Web pages:

Medieval Sourcebook: *www.fordham.edu/halsall/sbook2.html*

Ancient History Sourcebook: *www.fordham.edu/halsall/ancient/asbook.html*

LEADER GUIDE

A WORD TO LEADERS

Thank you for leading a group to equip believers in the critical field of apologetics through *Living in Truth: Confident Conversations in a Conflicted Culture*. In this leader guide you will find several elements.

For initial promotion and ongoing encouragement to members, I have included suggested entries for use in social media, email, and church bulletins. Think creatively about how you can encourage women to participate and to remain faithful.

The session suggestions provide for either six or seven group sessions. If you choose 7 sessions, you use the introductory first session to get acquainted, distribute member books, and begin to discuss the need in our culture for conversations on truth. If you choose to have 6 sessions, you will need to enroll group members and get them their books so they can study the first week's homework before the first group meeting. The group pages that begin each week will guide your group for the six sessions. Each week you will be discussing and seeking to apply the ideas from that week's homework. Note that while this is a print study, we have made some short introductory videos to introduce each of the group sessions. You will find group and promotional videos at *www.lifeway.com/LivingInTruth*.

The group pages will assist members to discuss the daily study that makes up each week's homework. The group page provides discussion questions for the session. Supplement these with your own study. Do not feel that you must cover all of the suggested group questions They serve as only a guide. You know your group best. Prayerfully choose learning activities most helpful to your group. In all faith conversations let dependence on the Holy Spirit be your guide.

Keep in mind that the real purpose of the group is to equip believers with conversation skills to discuss their faith and the truth of the gospel. The group will be successful to the degree that members wind up having good conversations with those outside the faith. Therefore plan your lesson strategy with that goal in mind. You may choose to spend group-session time processing the questions from your member books, or you may choose to develop your own lesson-plan strategy. The important question is: what will help you and your group members to develop the skill set and knowledge necessary to become more effective at having confident conversations about truth?

PROMOTING THE GROUP

Pray about how you can involve believers in this study. Nothing takes the place of personal invitation. Start early and enlist some influencers. Then encourage them to talk to others about participating in the study. Here are some social media and bulletin posts. Adapt them or develop you own to promote participation.

SAMPLE POSTS FOR SOCIAL MEDIA

New Study! "Be tolerant;" "Don't be a hater;" "Who are you to judge?" We're learning to respond to these in gentleness and respect. #LivinginTruth Mon 10/15 @7pm Rm 112

(Fill your date, time, and location)

New Study! Our culture struggles with what is true and how to know truth. We're doing a study on discussing truth in a conflicted culture. Come join us! Mon. 10/15 @7pm Rm 112

New Study by @maryjosharp, "Living In Truth: Confident Conversation in a Conflicted Culture." Come join us! Mon 10/15 @7pm Rm 112 #apologetics

CHURCH BULLETIN ANNOUNCEMENT:

We're becoming a culture that says no truth can be found about God. We also think that tolerance means accepting every view as equally true but—excluding the Christian faith. Christians are rapidly becoming the target of secular media and aggressive atheist propaganda, marginalizing not just Christian beliefs, but also Christian people.

Many women need a strengthened confidence in their beliefs in God in order to shine like stars in a misguided generation. This study will help Christians effectively converse on truth by following basic steps: 1) See the need for conversations on truth, 2) Know what you believe, 3) Listen to discover the cultural view, 4) Question cultural views and individual beliefs, 5) Respond to cultural views, and 6) Engage in a lifestyle of total truth.

The learning begins Mon. 10/15 @7pm in Rm 112.

Contact_____ for more information.

WEEK ONE

I suggest that you organize your group meetings around one of the following three themes. Prayerfully choose your theme and use the suggestions to begin conversations in the group each week. Consider using one of the following three themes for your group.

BATTLESHIP VERSUS CRUISE SHIP THEME: WHICH SHIP IS YOUR CHRISTIAN LIFE?

You could begin the study with a sea captain's hat. Print invitations in the form of cruise tickets and military appointment letters. Tell students the different invitations represent the two different vessels of truth Christians seem to occupy.

Throughout the study, add elements to the two-ship theme to show that as we add knowledge of authority and listening skills to uncover cultural untruths, we are adding to our battleship, not to the cruise ship. Consider offering contrasting imagery each week. For example ask, "What could we add to our battleship to represent trusting in Jesus as an authority?" or "What could we add to our cruise ship to represent trusting in faulty authorities?"

DOCTOR THEME: DIAGNOSING CULTURAL UNTRUTHS

You could begin the study with a white doctor's coat and add elements to your ensemble as you go along: glasses for seeing, head mirror for illuminating knowledge, stethoscope for listening, clipboard for asking questions, prescription bottles for responding, and an apple for engaging in total truth (an apple a day keeps the doctor away). Don't feel constrained by my suggestions! Have fun and be creative.

TOOL BELT THEME

If you have previously studied, *Why Do You Believe That?*, you might consider adding to your tool belt or expanding your tool belt to a toolbox!

BEFORE THE SESSION EACH WEEK:

- Pray for your group members
- Complete the homework for that week
- Prepare your battleship/cruise ship, doctor, or tool belt illustration for the week. For Week One this will involve the initial introduction of the idea.
- If you are using the battleship imagery you can call wear a sea captain's hat and/or uniform, bring posters of a battleship and cruise ship, set up models of a battleship and cruise ship. If you are using the doctor imagery, you can wear a white doctor's lab coat. If you are using the tool belt, bring your tool belt, or a tool box, or other tool related imagery.

SOCIAL MEDIA INVITES AND REMINDERS:

LIT Wk 1: This week, we're setting sail on our journey. Come join us! Mon. 10/15 @7pm Rm 112 #LivingInTruth **(Remember to include your date, time, and location)**

LIT Wk 1: Our culture struggles with what is true and how to know truth. We're doing a study on discussing truth in a conflict culture. Come join us! Mon. 10/15 @7pm Rm 112 #LivingInTruth

LIT Wk 1: Why we should discuss #truth? Truth impacts all of us. Come join the conversation this week. Mon 10/15 @7pm Rm 112 #LivingInTruth

LIT Wk 1: Why discuss truth? Because our culture is becoming more intolerant. Come join our study on truth conversations. Mon 10/15 @7pm Rm 112 #LivingInTruth

LIT Wk 1: Why discuss truth? As Jesus' followers we are to be lovers of the truth. Come join our study on discussing truth in a conflict culture. Mon 10/15 @7pm Rm 112 #LivingInTruth

EMAIL:

Hey (friends, ladies, crew, classmates),

This week we begin our journey of *Living in Truth*. As the study states, "my hope in working through this study is that you will discover a renewed and refreshed desire to know the truth—who is a living Person." We will engage in answering the untruths that have kept us from having effective conversation about God in our public lives. As the author states, "I pray you will begin to find the freedom in Christ that is already yours to openly discuss your beliefs, no matter how conflicted our culture becomes." I'm so excited to begin this journey with you!

See you Mon. 10/15 @7pm Rm 112!

WEEK TWO

BEFORE THE SESSION

- Pray for each group member

- Pray that your group members will have opportunities for great conversations about God

- Complete Week Two homework

- Prepare your battleship/cruise ship, doctor, or tool belt illustration for this week.

- If you are using the battleship imagery discuss the importance of chain of command and why the captain is seen as an authority. You can also bring in a schematic of a battleship and discuss how true knowledge of the ship helps you in your assignment onboard. Further, you can set up false authorities on your cruise ship. If you are using the doctor imagery, today is the day for your head mirror to illuminate the truth (to know). If you are using the tool belt or box, bring a tool that represents knowing your beliefs (recognizing proper authority).

SOCIAL MEDIA INVITES AND REMINDERS:

LIT Wk 2: This week, we're learning about trusting Jesus as an authority. Come join us! Mon. 10/15 @7pm Rm 112 #LivingInTruth **(Remember to include your date, time, and location)**

LIT Wk 2: This week we're learning to build our lives on the foundation of Jesus, rather than on the shifting sands of culture. Mon 10/15 @7pm Rm 112 #LivingInTruth

LIT Wk 2: What are you trusting as an authority and why? Come join us this week for "Living in Truth." Mon 10/15 @7pm Rm 112 #LivingInTruth

LIT Wk 2: Know what you believe. Join us for week two of "Living in Truth." Mon 10/15 @7p Rm 112 #LivingInTruth

EMAIL:

Hey (friends, ladies, crew, classmates),

This week we continue our journey of *Living in Truth*. We will engage in answering the untruths that have kept us from having effective conversation about God in our public lives. I pray you will begin to find the freedom in Christ that is already yours to openly discuss your beliefs, no matter how conflicted our culture becomes. I'm so glad to share this journey with you!

See you Mon. 10/15 @7pm Rm. 112!

WEEK THREE

BEFORE THE SESSION

- Pray for each group member

- Pray that your group members will have opportunities for great conversations about God

- Complete Week Three homework

- Prepare your battleship/cruise ship, doctor, or tool belt illustration for this week.

- If you are using the battleship imagery you can discuss the importance of hearing and obeying the captain. Think of how you can convey the importance of listening as a soldier on a battleship. Further, you can set up a contrast with the people on a cruise ship, who may or may not be attentive to the captain's instructions. If you are using the doctor imagery, today is the day for your stethoscope for hearing the truth. If you are using the tool belt or box, bring a tool that you feel represents listening (or an upgraded version of the listening tool used during *Why Do You Believe That?*).

SOCIAL MEDIA INVITES AND REMINDERS:

LIT Wk 3: This week, we're learning to listen to discover what people believe. Come join us! Mon. 10/15 @7pm Rm 112 #LivingInTruth **(Remember to include your date, time, and location)**

LIT Wk 3: Come discover how we can impact our culture by listening well! Mon 10/15 @7pm Rm 112 #LivingInTruth

LIT Wk 3: Are you hearing the difference between objective and subjective statements? We'll discover this important difference this Mon 10/15 @7pm Rm 112 #LivingInTruth

LIT: Listen well. Our conversations are greatly altered by our listening ability. Join us for week 3 of "Living in Truth." Mon 10/15 @7p Rm 112 #LivingInTruth

EMAIL:

Hey (friends, ladies, crew, classmates),

Since we live in a time in which our society is so conflicted about the truth, we must learn to listen to discover what people actually believe. Listening well to others is a vital part of having effective conversations. This week, we will not only address how to listen well, but we will also address two different types of statements, subjective and objective. As we learn to hear the difference between these kinds of statements, we'll begin to understand how these statements greatly affect our conversations. We'll look at why people are sometimes offended by our truth conversation about God because of confusion due to subjectivity versus objectivity. This is an exciting week for opening up the conversation on God!

See you Mon. 10/15 @7pm Rm 112!

WEEK FOUR

BEFORE THE SESSION

- Pray for each group member

- Pray that your group members will have opportunities for great conversations about God

- Pray for your group's understanding of important issues covered this week

- Complete Week Four homework

- Prepare your battleship/cruise ship, doctor, or tool belt illustration for this week.

- If you are using the battleship imagery you can discuss the importance of asking clarifying questions rather than making assumptions based upon another crew member's statement or about how a piece of equipment works on the battleship. Further, you can set up a contrast with the people on cruise ship, who may have heard something wrong and, instead of asking questions, acted upon a wrong assumption. If you are using the doctor imagery, today is the day for your clipboard for asking questions to discern truth. If you are using the tool belt or box, bring a tool that is a diagnostic instrument (plumb line, level, scale, etc.).

SOCIAL MEDIA INVITES AND REMINDERS:

LIT Wk 4: This week, we're learning about science & faith, good & evil, and tolerance. Come join us! Mon. 10/15 @7pm Rm 112 #LivingInTruth **(Remember to include your date, time, and location)**

LIT Wk 4: Come discover questions we can ask when facing tough issues concerning belief in God. Mon 10/15 @7pm Rm 112 #LivingInTruth

LIT Wk 4: Christians should ask a lot more questions when confronted with hot topics in our culture. We'll discover some this week: Mon 10/15 @7pm Rm 112 #LivingInTruth

LIT Wk 4: Ask questions for clarification. Our conversations are greatly improved when understand the other person's point-of-view. Join us for week 4 of "Living in Truth." Mon 10/15 @7p Rm 112 #LivingInTruth

EMAIL:

Hey (friends, ladies, crew, classmates),

Week Four is a good reminder that we need to ask more questions about the things we see and hear in our society. There are many conflicted messages about truth that can make a person feel intimidated to engage in conversation at all. Questions provide us with a means of better understanding an individual's beliefs, aid in avoidance of assumptions, and therefore help us better minister to people. This week we learn questions we should ask when engaging in the topics of science & faith, good and evil, and intolerance. We will also practice conversation on heated topics. It's going to be another great week for conversations!

See you Mon. 10/15 @7pm Rm 112!

WEEK FIVE

BEFORE THE SESSION

- Pray for each group member by name

- Complete Week Five homework

- There are a few mock-dialogs this week. Prepare your group by letting them know in advance that you will be engaging in these mock conversations this week.

- Prepare your battleship/cruise ship, doctor, or tool belt illustration for this week: we are going to respond to cultural untruths and individual beliefs about God

- If you are using the battleship imagery you can call for "all hands on deck" or put soldiers on your ship in battle positions. If you are using the doctor imagery, you can discuss that you will be prescribing medicine to handle false beliefs about Christians and Christianity. If you are using the tool belt, bring a tool that represents fixing a certain problem.

SOCIAL MEDIA INVITES AND REMINDERS:

LIT Wk 5: This week, we're learning responses to some misconceptions about Christianity. Come join us! Mon. 10/15 @7pm Rm 112 #LivingInTruth **(Remember to include your date, time, and location)**

LIT Wk 5: "Christians are ignorant & hypocritical." What would you say in response? Learn some responses this week! Mon. 10/15 @7pm Rm 112 #LivingInTruth

LIT Wk 5: Ever heard that the Bible is a man-made myth? Let's learn to respond to this claim this week. Mon 10/15 @7pm Rm 112 #LivingInTruth

EMAIL:

Hey (friends, ladies, crew, classmates),

We face some challenging misconceptions about Christianity and Christians. This week we will learn to respond to the statements that Christians are ignorant, Christians are hypocrites, and that the Bible is a man-made myth. We'll also discuss some reasons for why people think these things are true. I know this is going to be an exciting week as we directly engage the conflicted messages of our culture.

See you Mon. 10/15 @7pm Rm 112!

WEEK SIX

BEFORE THE SESSION

- Pray for each group member by name

- Complete Week Six homework

- Prepare your battleship/cruise ship, doctor, or tool belt illustration for this week: we are going to make a commitment to recognizing the sacred/secular split and releasing ourselves from this cultural dogma to the freedom in Christ

- If you are using the battleship imagery you can commission your soldiers or give them medals for engaging nobly in battle. If you are using the doctor imagery, you can begin the session on crutches (representing the sacred/secular split) and then put the crutches down as you discuss freedom in Christ. If you are using the tool belt, bring in a tool that represents freedom. Perhaps, research one tool that represents advancement in technology freeing mankind up to build things better and faster.

SOCIAL MEDIA INVITES AND REMINDERS:

LIT Wk 6: This week, we're learning that we are not bound by cultural untruths. Come join us! Mon. 10/15 @7pm Rm 112 #LivingInTruth **(Remember to include your date, time, and location)**

LIT Wk 6: It's our last session together! Come be encouraged to live in Christ's freedom in a culture of confusion. See you there! Mon. 10/15 @7pm Rm 112 #LivingInTruth

LIT Wk 6: Last LIT session this week! See you there! Mon 10/15 @7pm Rm 112 #LivingInTruth

EMAIL:

Hey (friends, ladies, crew, classmates),

As we come to the end of our study, *Living in Truth*, I want to hear about how God has used this study in your life. Has your perspective changed on conversations? If so, how? Have you already engaged in a conversation that you'd like to share with us? How did this study help reinforce what you already knew to do in conversation? What else has God been doing since we began? Let's use our last group time together to encourage one another through story, prayer, and great conversation!

See you Mon. 10/15 @7pm Rm 112!

WEEK 1

1. Adapted from "Why are Christians so arrogant?" Available from the Internet: *http://chatpilot-godisamyth.blogspot.com.*

2. Friedrich Nietzsche, *Thus Spake Zarathustra: A Book for All and None*, Trans. Thomas Common (New York: The Macmillan Company, 1911), 239.

3. Dallas Willard, as quoted in *Christian Apologetics Past and Present From 1500: A Primary Source Reader*. Vol. 2. Eds. William Edgar, K. Scott Oliphint (Wheaton, IL: Crossway, 2011), 650.

4. "Truth," *Merriam-Webster Online Dictionary*, Merriam-Webster, Inc. Available from the Internet: *www.merriam-webster.com*

5. Aristotle, *Metaphysics* (Stilwell, KS: Digireads.com Publishing, 2006), 44.

6. Francis A. Schaeffer, *How Should We Then Live?* (Wheaton, IL: Crossway, 2005) and Allan Bloom, *The Closing of the American Mind* (New York, NY: Simon & Schuster, 1987).

7. Gerald L. Borchert, *New American Commentary—John 12-21* Vol 25b (Nashville: B&H Publishing), Word Search Software.

8. William Hendriksen and Simon J. Kistemaker, *Baker New Testament Commentary – Exposition of the First Epistle to the Corinthians*. (Baker Academic), WordSearch Software.

9. Saint Augustine. *Confessions* (Oxford: Oxford Press, 1992), 200.

10. J.B. Phillips, *The New Testament in Modern English* (HarperCollins, 1962), Romans 12:1-2.

11. Rob Cooper, "Forcing a religion on your child is as bad as child abuse, claims atheist professor Richard Dawkins," [online] April 2013. Available from the Internet: *dailymail.com.*

12. The above material was paraphrased and/or directly quoted from Nancy Pearcey, *Total Truth: Liberating Christianity from Its Cultural Captivity* (Wheaton, IL: Crossway Books, 2005), 20-21, 101-106.

WEEK 2

1. Albert Einstein, "Quote Investigator," [online, cited September 1 2014]. Available from the Internet: *quoteinvestigator.com*

2. Hendriksen and Kistemaker, *Baker New Testament Commentary*, WordSearch Software.

3. Max Anders, Stuart Weber, *Holman New Testament Commentary—Matthew* (B&H Publishing Group), WordSearch Software.

4. *The New Schaff-Herzog Encyclopedia of Religious Knowledge*, Vol. IV, (New York and London: Funk and Wagnalls Company, 1909), 269.

5. Billy Graham, available on the Internet: *www.goodreads.com*

6. Weber and Anders, *Holman New Testament Commentary—Matthew,* WordSearch Software.

7. Dallas Willard. *The Divine Conspiracy.* (New York: Harper Collins), 48-49.

8. Weber and Anders, *Holman New Testament Commentary—Matthew,* WordSearch Software.

9. Ian Hutchinson, Professor of Nuclear Science and Engineering, Alcator C-Mod Tokamak Plasma Confinement Experiment Co-Principal, Massachusetts Institute of Technology. Veritas Forum Lecture. Available from: *http://questions.veritas.org/science-faith/scientism/what-is-science-and-what-is-scientism*. Accessed June 9, 2015.

10. John Lennox, "Can Faith and Science Coexist? Mathematician and Christian John Lennox Responds." Scientific American blog. Available from: *blogs.scientificamerican.com*. Accessed June 9, 2015.

11. Scientific American. "Nobel Laureate Harry Kroto: The Threatened Enlightenment." Available from: *www.scientificamerican.com*. Accessed June 9, 2015.

12. Andrew Brown, "Science is the Only Road to Truth? Don't be Absurd." *The Guardian*. Available from: http://www.theguardian.com. Accessed June 9, 2015.

13. J.P. Moreland, *Scaling the Secular City: A Defense of Christianity* (Grand Rapids, MI: Baker Books, 1987), 197.

14. Ibid., 198.

15. Ibid.

16. "Ten Quick Responses to Atheist Claims." *Christianity Today.* Available from: http://www.christianitytoday.com. Accessed June 9, 2015.

17. John Polkinghorne and Frank Tipler, adapted from David Wood and Nabeel Qureshi. "Common Muslim Objections." PowerPoint 2009.

WEEK 3

1. Weber and Anders, *Holman New Testament Commentary—Matthew,* WordSearch Software.

2. Tim Muehloff, *I Beg to Differ* (Downers Grove, IL: InterVarsity Press, 2014), 89.

3. Tremper Longman III and Raymond B. Dillard, *An Introduction to the Old Testament* (Grand Rapids, MI: Zondervan, 2006), 447-448.

4. Ibid.

5. Neil Carter, "Apologetics isn't for the lost, it's for the saved," Patheos [online], 12 October 2014 [cited October 25 2014]. Available from the Internet: *www.patheos.com*.

6. Ken Sande, *The Peacemaker*, 3rd ed. (Grand Rapids, MI: Baker Books, 2004), 168-169.

7. Jason Blevins, "Feds chase criminal case against artist who marred rocks in parks," *The Denver Post* [online], 23 October 2014 [cited November 11 2014]. Available from the Internet: *www.denverpost.com*.

8. Lane Moore, "Female Graffiti Artist Is the New Most-Hated Person On Instagram: And possibly your new hero," Cosmopolitan [online] 24 October 2014 [cited November 11 2014]. Available from the Internet: *www.cosmopolitan.com*.

9. G.K. Chesterton and Denis Conlin, *The Collected Works of G.K. Chesterton*, Volume 14 (San Francisco: Ignatius Press, 1993), 350.

10. William Lane Craig, "The Problem of Evil." Reasonable Faith Website. Available from: http://www.reasonablefaith.org/the-problem-of-evil. Accessed June 25, 2015.

11. Quote by St. Augustine of Hippo.

12. Douglas Groothius, *Christian Apologetics* (Downers Grove, IL: InterVarsity Press, 2011), 356.

13. *River Out of Eden: A Darwinian View of Life* (New York: Harper Collins, 1995), 133.

14. Lou Markos, *Apologetics for the 21st Century* (Wheaton: Crossway, 2010), 142.

15. William Lane Craig, "The Problem of Evil."

WEEK 4

1. Weber and Anders, *Holman New Testament Commentary—Matthew,* WordSearch Software.

2. Tim Muelhoff, *I Beg to Differ: Navigating Difficult Conversations With Truth and Love* (Downers Grove: InterVarsity Press, 2014), 103.

3. Patterson, Grenny, McMillian, and Switzler, *Crucial Conversations: Tools for Talking When Stakes are High* (Chicago: McGraw-Hill, 2012), 55.

4. Tim Muelhoff, *I Beg to Differ: Navigating Difficult Conversations With Truth and Love*, 103.

5. "empirical," *www.merriam-webster.com/dictionary/empirical.* Accessed September 12, 2014.

7. Julian Baginni, "Yes, Life Without God can be Bleak: Atheism is About Facing up to That" from *The Guardian.* [online article] Available at: *http://www.guardian.co.uk.* Accessed October 30, 2012.

8. Randy Newman, *Questioning Evangelism* (Grand Rapids: Kregel Publications, 2004), 29.

9. Read more from *The Globe and Mail*, "B.C. Revokes Consent for Controversial Law School," http://bit.ly/12TBKF1 and from the *CBC News* "Trinity Western Law School Accreditation Denial Upheld by Ontario Court," http://bit.ly/1dHOiET).

10. C.S. Lewis, *The Abolition of Man* (New York: HarperOne, 1944), 59.

11. "hate speech," *http://definitions.uslegal.com/h/hate-speech/.* Accessed July 14, 2015.

WEEK 5

1. "Loaded Words: Vocabulary That Packs a Punch in Persuasive Writing," Read.Write.Think website. Available from: *http://www.readwritethink.org/classroom-resources/lesson-plans.*

2. *Baker New Testament Commentary,* "Exposition of James, Epistles of John, Peter, and Jude." WordSearch Software, Accessed January 25, 2015.

3. David Gooding and John Lennox, *Christianity: Opium or Truth?* Available from: http://www.keybibleconcepts.org. Accessed June 25, 2015.

4. Ibid.

5. Ibid.

6. Frederick Copleston, *A History of Philosophy,* Vol. 1, "Greece and Rome" (New York: Doubleday, 1993, 1962), 11.

7. John N. Oswalt, *The Bible among the Myths: Unique Revelation or Just Ancient Literature?* (Grand Rapids: Zondervan, 2009), Kindle Edition.

8. Ibid.

9. G.K. Chesterton, G.K. Chesterton on Literature." Cambridge Study Center. Available from the Internet: *www. CambridgeStudyCenter.com.*

10. Adapted from Richard Dawkins. *The God Delusion* (New York: Transworld Publishers, 2006), 77.

11. Dennis Ingolfsland, "The Historical Jesus," [online, cited September 1 2007]. Available from the Internet: *www. knowjesus.com.*

12. The Jesus Seminar is a group of seventy-five plus scholars who meet twice a year to make pronouncements about the historical Jesus. They are comprised of liberal Catholics and Protestants, Jews, and atheists.

13. John Dominic Crossan, *Jesus: A Revolutionary Biography* (New York: HarperCollins, 1994), 145.

14. Gary Habermas, "The Minimal Facts Approach to the Resurrection of Jesus: The Role of Methodology as a Crucial Component in Establishing Historicity," [online], 2 August 2012, [cited July 1, 2015]. Available from the Internet: *www.garyhabermas.com.*

15. Paul L. Maier, In the Fullness of Time: A Historian Looks at Christmas, Easter, and the Early Church (San Francisco: Harper Collins, 1991), 197.

16. John Warwick Montgomery, *History and Christianity* (San Bernardino, CA: Here's Life Publishers 1983), 43.20. Norman Anderson.

17. Sir James Norman Anderson, *Christianity and the World Religions* (Leicester, England: Inter-Varsity Press, 1984), 53.

WEEK 6

1. Nancy Pearcey, *Total Truth: Liberating Christianity from Its Cultural Captivity* (Wheaton, IL: Crossway Books, 2004), 20.

2. Ibid.

3. Ibid.

4. *Baker New Testament Commentary.* "Exposition of the Gospel According to Matthew." WordSearch Software. (Accessed February 16, 2015)

5. *Baker New Testament Commentary.* "Exposition of the Gospel According to John." Word Search Software.

6. C.S. Lewis, *The Problem of Pain* (New York: HarperCollins Publishers, Inc., 1996, 1940), 48.

7. Ibid.

8. Francis Bacon, *The New Organon.* trans. Jonathan Bennett. Available from: *http://www.earlymoderntexts.com/ authors/bacon.* Accessed June 28, 2015.

9. Nancy Pearcey, *Total Truth: Liberating Christianity from Its Cultural Captivity* (Wheaton: Crossway Books, 2005), 118.

10. Ibid., 121.

11. Ferrari slogan adapted from "5 Most Inspirational Car Slogans." Available from: *http://blog.appnova.com/5-inspirational-car-slogans/*. Accessed June 29, 2015.

12. Ken Sande, *The Peacemaker* (Grand Rapids: Baker Books, 1991), 165.

13. Nancy Pearcey, *Total Truth: Liberating Christianity from Its Cultural Captivity,* adapted from page 38.

14. Ibid., adapted from 38-39.

15. Timothy Freke and Peter Gandy, *The Jesus Mysteries: Was the "Original Jesus" a Pagan God?* (New York: Three Rivers Press, 1999). Payam Nabarz, *The Mysteries of Mithras: The Pagan Belief That Shaped the Christian World* (Rochester: Inner Traditions, 2005). *The Historical Jesus: Five Views,* eds. James K. Beilby and Paul Rhodes Eddy (Downers Grove, IL: InterVarsity Press, 2009).

16. I don't wish to assume motives, but this contravention of fact is so egregious on behalf of the argument's proponents, such as "Zeitgeist, the Movie," that it causes me to wonder about the author's intent.

17. This study was first published on The Apologetics Guy blog: *www.apologeticsguy.com/blog/*

notes

notes

notes

notes

notes

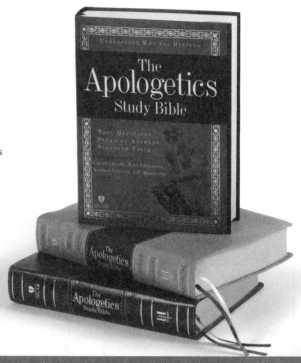

talk amongst yourselves

Stop by
Our Online
Home

We have resources to help you grow in your faith, develop as a leader, and encourage you as you go. Visit us online to find Bible studies, digital downloads, events, and more!

lifeway.com/women